A Kayaker's Guide to the

Hudson River Valley
The Quieter Waters
Rivers, Creeks, Lakes and Ponds

Shari Aber

Every creature is better alive than dead, men and moose and pine trees, and he who understands it aright will rather preserve its life than destroy it.

Henry David Thoreau

A Kayaker's Guide to the

Hudson River Valley
The Quieter Waters
Rivers, Creeks, Lakes and Ponds

Shari Aber

BLACK·DOME

Published by

Black Dome Press Corp.
1011 Route 296, Hensonville, New York 12439
www.blackdomepress.com
Tel: (518) 734–6357

ISBN-13: 978-1-883789-53-4
ISBN-10: 1-883789-53-2

Library of Congress Cataloging-in-Publication Data

Aber, Shari.

A Kayaker's Guide to the Hudson River Valley: the quieter waters: rivers, creeks, lakes, and
ponds / Shari Aber.
      p. cm.
   Includes bibliographical references.
   ISBN-13: 978-1-883789-53-4

   ISBN-10: 1-883789-53-2
   1. Kayaking—Hudson River Valley (N.Y. and N.J.)—Guidebooks. 2. Hudson River Valley
(N.Y. and N.J.)—Guidebooks. I. Title.

   GV776.H83A34 2007
   797.122′4097473--dc22
                              2007007999

**Outdoor recreational activities are by their very nature potentially hazardous and contain
risk. See pages 16 and 17.**

Maps created with DeLorme software © 2006 DeLorme (www.delorme.com) Topo USA®
"Fishing on the Susquehanna in July" from *Picnic, Lightning*, by Billy Collins ©
   1998. Reprinted by permission of the University of Pittsburgh Press.
"Types of Kayaks" courtesy of www.kayakhelp.com.
"Back Bay" © 2000 by Jean Valla McAvoy. Used with permission.
Author photograph by Joseph Ferri.
"Bald Eagle in Flight" cover photograph by Larry Federman.
All other photographs are by the author.

Design: Toelke Associates, www.toelkeassociates.com

Printed in the USA

10 9 8 7 6 5 4 3 2 1

Dedication

For my big brother, Joel, who in our backyard in
the city first revealed to me the surprises of nature.
He would have loved to paddle the rivers and
backwaters, to see the eagles again diving over the
Hudson, to glimpse the green heron posed still,
silent, watching over the marsh.

And for Joe, who has offered always his unwavering
support.

Contents

KEY: GREENE, ULSTER, COLUMBIA, AND DUTCHESS

Greene County

G-1 Catskill Creek

G-2 Dubois Creek

G-3 RamsHorn Creek

G-4 CD Lane Park

G-5 Colgate Lake

G-6 Green Lake

G-7 North-South Lake

Columbia County

C-1 Stockport Creek

C-2 Stockport Flats

C-3 Copake Lake

C-4 Kinderhook Lake

C-5 Lake Taghkanic

C-6 Queechy Lake

Ulster County

U-1 Black Creek

U-2 Chodikee Lake

U-3 Esopus Creek

U-4 Mouth of Esopus Creek

U-5 Rondout Creek—
High Falls

U-6 Rondout Creek—
Eddyville

U-7 Rondout Creek—
Kingston

U-8 Wallkill River—
Wallkill to Walden

U-9 Wallkill River—
New Paltz to Rifton

U-10 Alder Lake

U-11 Lake Minnewaska

U-12 Onteora Lake

U-13 Tillson Lake

U-14 Upper Pond

U-15 Yankeetown Pond

Dutchess County

D-1 Fishkill Creek

D-2 The Mouth of the
Fishkill Creek

D-3 Tenmile River

D-4 Tivoli Bays

D-5 Wappinger Creek

D-6 The Mouth of the
Wappinger Creek

D-7 Rudd Pond

D-8 Stissing Pond

D-9 Sylvan Lake

D-10 Upton Lake

D-11 Wappinger Lake

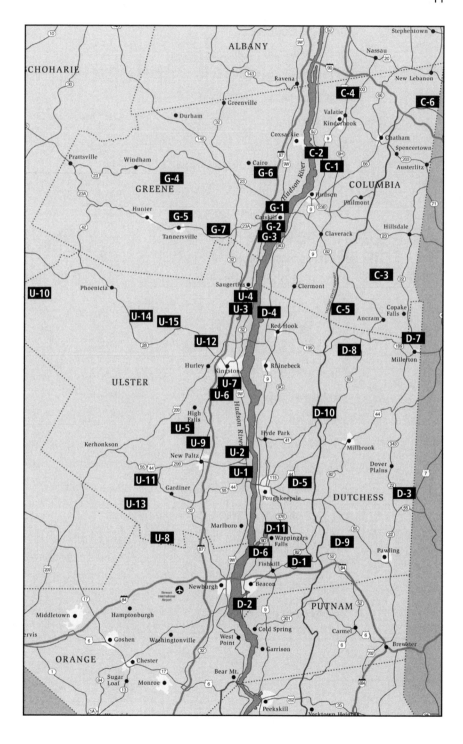

Orange County

O-1 Delaware River

O-2 Moodna Creek

O-3 Neversink River

O-4 Otter Kill

O-5 Wallkill River

O-6 Harriman State Park Lakes

O-7 Sterling Forest State Park Lakes

O-8 Winding Hills County Park

Putnam County

P-1 Constitution Marsh

P-2 East Branch Croton River—Green Chimneys

P-3 East Branch Croton River—Patterson

P-4 Canopus Lake

P-5 Stillwater Pond

P-6 White Pond

Sullivan County

S-1 Bashakill

S-2 Mongaup Falls Reservoir

S-3 Rio Reservoir

Sussex County, New Jersey

SX-1 Wallkill River National Wildlife Refuge

Rockland County

R-1 Lake Sebago

R-2 Lake Welch

Westchester County

W-1 Mohansic Lake

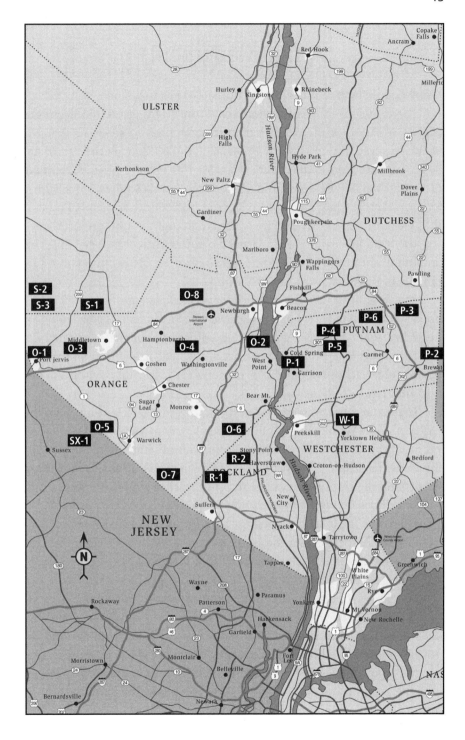

Acknowledgments

Many people helped me with this book. Thanks to you all.

There are those environmentalists, outfitters, acquaintances and friends who took time from their busy schedules to steer me towards waterways to explore—Evelyn Chiarito, Edie Keasbey, Beth Waterman, Scott Cuppett, Ron Rader, Laurie Fila, Sharon Pickett, private outfitters Ernie Gardner, Bill Kennedy, and Mark Price, Dennis Squires, Steve Schuyler, Dane Leroy, Chris Lucas, John Devine, and countless people I met on the creeks, lakes, and rivers who willingly shared their experiences.

There are those naturalists who led paddles through refuge lands and taught me about the local wildlife, geology and ecology—Jim Utter, Eric Lind, Jean McAvoy, and Larry Federman.

Thanks to those who generously allowed me to include their work in this book—Billy Collins for his poem, Jean McAvoy for her lyrics, Jakob Jelling for his webpage and Larry Federman for his cover photo of an eagle in flight.

Thanks to Pete Seeger, whose art is steeped in integrity and whose commitment to our region and our environment has revitalized our beautiful Hudson River.

Thanks to those who rekindled my commitment to writing: from the Hudson Valley Writing Project, Bonnie Kaplan, Tom Meyer, and Mary Sawyer; from the Lehigh Valley Writing Project—for that is where the seed for this book was planted—Nancy Coco; and from both National Writing Project sites, all the enthusiastic and supportive teacher-writers. Thanks to Ann LaMott, whose *Bird by Bird* philosophy helped me complete this book.

Thanks to those who helped the idea for this venture become a reality—Toelke Associates for the book design, editor Steve Hoare for his amazing technical expertise and publisher Debbie Allen for her patient attention to detail and confidence in me and the project.

Thanks to my longtime friend, scout co-leader and fellow amateur birder, Patti Lewis, who joined me on some of my adventures, and my daughters, Dara and Kendra, who sometimes paddled with me and on occasion served as a lifeline, bailing me out when I got in over my head.

And then there's Joe Ferri. He helped in so many ways—kayaking with me, reading and editing the manuscript, taking the flattering author photo and encouraging me from the start.

The Limitations of a Paddling Guide

When I was very small my parents rented a cabin on Tripp Pond in Poland, Maine. We went out one afternoon in a rowboat, my brother Joel and my dad rowing, my mom in the back and I in the prow. Dark thunderheads rolled in and with them a wind that churned up the calm water, creating whitecaps. The bank from which we had launched disappeared in a gray cloud. Lightning bolts struck the middle of the lake. My father pushed my brother aside, took over both oars, and pulled fast and fierce towards the nearest shore. I watched the rhythmic flexing of his arm muscles. Then his face tensed, tears clouded my mom's eyes, and I realized with absolute certainty that the boat was being blown towards lightning and the center of the roiling lake.

Spotting us and our plight, two fishermen in a motorboat sped to us, tied our boat to theirs and pulled us to safety. Not so much the rescue, but the event itself taught me some important lessons—lessons about life and lessons about water. I learned about the vulnerability of even the strongest people in the world—in this case, my parents. I learned about the ferocious power of nature in the raw. I learned about the deception of language, how naming an over 700-acre body of water a "pond" lulled us into believing it benign.

Quite recently one October day I returned to Putnam County intending to revisit the Croton River heading towards the East Branch Reservoir. In the spring Joe and I had paddled easily southward two or three miles. I wanted to go back, kayak another couple of miles, and approach the reservoir to see how New York City marked the boundary, information I would include in the Green Chimneys write-up. The narrowness of the river, with its now clearly demarked shoreline, struck me immediately—far different from the flooded lake-like body of water sprawling over its boundaries that we'd seen a few months earlier. Now, plants drying out and dying back crowded its raised banks, banks our boats had glided over after the spring rains. Beaver dams and fallen trees impeded our progress every hundred feet. Not wanting to get wet in the now chill water, I gave up and headed back.

And so this word of warning. While I have kayaked every creek and river included in this guide and can attest to the course I found, I cannot vouch for forces of nature: a tree, its root structure weakened by floods, knocked over by wind, blocking the river flow; a beaver dam destroyed by floodwaters. I cannot vouch for seasonal changes: snow melt; spring rains; summer droughts. Trips on the wider and deeper bodies of water included in this book—those on the Hudson, the Delaware, the Esopus, the Rondout, the Wallkill, the mouths of the various creeks, and all the lakes—are only minimally and gradually affected by the ravages of nature. But weather conditions and natural events frequently impact the course of the narrower creeks and rivers. With the anticipation of the unexpected, the very volatility of nature imbues these trips with an aura of mystery. View them as adventures, but be prepared if necessary to turn your kayak around and head back, postponing the trip for another day.

Caution

Outdoor recreational activities are by their very nature potentially hazardous and contain risk. All participants in such activities must assume responsibility for their own actions and safety. No book can be a substitute for good judgment. The outdoors is forever changing. The authors and the publisher cannot be held responsible for inaccuracies, errors, or omissions, or for any changes in the details of this publication, or for the consequences of any reliance on the information contained herein, or for the safety of people in the outdoors.

Safety Tips

Precaution against drowning:
- You should wear your personal flotation device (PFD or life jacket) at all times when in the kayak, even if you swim well. This is especially true when in water with a current, since the PFD will float away if the boat capsizes.
- If you fall into moving water, point your feet downstream so that they take the brunt of a collision with any obstacle.

Precaution against hypothermia:

- You may get wet when kayaking. Wear quick-drying clothes and have a change of clothing in your vehicle. Shoes that shed water quickly are advisable. If you think you will be portaging, wear shoes that also offer support and have soles that grip.

Precaution against weather-related problems:

- Check the weather before you go out. You do not want to be on open water during thunderstorms.
- Check tide charts before going on the Hudson River. You generally want to explore the marsh areas adjacent to the Hudson during mid to high tides. If you are paddling the river itself, consider taking advantage of the current. The Hudson is tidal. This means that when the tide is coming in, the river flows northward. As the tide goes out, the current shifts and the river flows south. Be sure to check the charts for the area where you will be paddling. High tide is significantly later near Albany than it is near New York City. Several Web sites provide tide data for the Hudson:

  http://www.hudsonriver.com/tides.htm
  http://www.noreast.com/TidesNew/SelectLocation.
      cfm?CurrentIndex=511&IndexHistory=952%2C33
  http://www.hrfanj.org/river_conditions.htm

- Be aware of recent precipitation and water levels. In flood conditions, even flatwater rivers and creeks can develop strong and dangerous currents.

Overall precaution:

Let someone know where you intend to kayak. Take a cell phone and protect it in a watertight bag or container. Go out and enjoy—with a paddling partner.

Paddles by Difficulty

The rating system in this book takes into consideration a number of factors: the simplicity of trip planning; the ease of the launch; the amount of current; the presence of riffles and rapids; the length of the trip; the size and volatility of the body of water; the condition and maintenance of the area; and the necessity of portages. Thus an "easy" trip should have a relatively trouble-free launch and require one vehicle. The waterway should be generally maintained well. Fallen trees (deadfall) should rarely if ever cause difficulty, and no portages should be required. The water should have little or no current; a novice kayaker should be able to paddle out and back with no problem. The likely number and difficulty of the challenges of a trip determine its rating. Thus, the more challenges faced in a given paddle and the more hazardous the challenges, the higher the rating. The letters immediately following the difficulty designation for each trip indicate the rationale for the particular rating given. You may not encounter the indicated challenges. Care has been taken to err on the side of caution. Remember, however, there are no guarantees. Winds can, for example, make a calm body of water choppy. A tree can fall blocking a normally clear creek, necessitating a portage.

A	Access challenging
R	Riffles
L	Low-hanging branches
D	Deadfall
P	Portages
CH	Choppy
C	Current may be strong
O	One-way trip
M	Moving flat water
W	White water

Weather conditions and natural events can and do impact the waterways. See caution on pages 16 and 17.

Easy

Dutchess County
Fishkill Creek in Brinckerhoff
Rudd Pond in Millerton
Stissing Pond in Pine Plains
Sylvan Lake in Beekman
Upton Lake in Stanford
Wappinger Lake
 in Wappingers Falls

Orange County
Blue Lake in Warwick
Island Pond in Tuxedo
Lake Askoti in Tuxedo
Lake Kanawauke in Tuxedo
Lake Skannatati in Tuxedo
Lake Stahahe in Tuxedo
Lake Tiorati in Tuxedo
Little Dam Lake in Tuxedo
Otter Kill in Washingtonville
Silver Mine Lake in Woodbury
Winding Hills County Park
 in Montgomery

Putnam County
Canopus Lake in Philipstown
Stillwater Pond in Putnam Valley
White Pond in Kent

Ulster County
Alder Lake in Hardenburgh
Black Creek in Lloyd
Chodikee Lake in Highland

Lake Minnewaska in Gardiner
Onteora Lake in Kingston
Rondout Creek in the High Falls
 Area—High Falls South
Tillson Lake in Gardiner
Upper Pond in Woodstock
Wallkill River from
 Wallkill to Walden
Wallkill River from
 New Paltz to Rifton
Yankeetown Pond in Woodstock

Columbia County
Copake Lake in Copake
Kinderhook Lake in Niverville
Lake Taghkanic in Ancram
Queechy Lake in Canaan

Greene County
CD Lane Park in Windham
Colgate Lake in East Jewett
Green Lake in Athens
North-South Lake in Haines Falls

Rockland County
Lake Sebago in Pomona
Lake Welch in Stony Point

Sullivan County
The Bashakill
Mongaup Falls Reservoir
 in Forestburgh
Rio Reservoir in Forestburgh

Westchester County

Mohansic Lake
  in Yorktown Heights

Easy to Moderate

The Mouth of the Wappinger
  Creek in Wappingers Falls
  (Dutchess)
East Branch Croton River
  Starting from Green Chimneys
  (Putnam)
Esopus Creek from the Village
  of Saugerties towards Kingston
  (Ulster)
Rondout Creek in Eddyville
  (Ulster)

Moderate

Tivoli Bays in Red Hook
  (Dutchess)
Wappinger Creek from Pleasant
  Valley to Poughkeepsie
  (Dutchess)
Moodna Creek and Marsh
  in New Windsor (Orange)
Constitution Marsh in
  Cold Spring (Putnam)
East Branch Croton River from
  Patterson to Green Chimneys
  (Putnam)
The Mouth of the Esopus Creek
  in Saugerties (Ulster)
Rondout Creek in Kingston
  (Ulster)

Stockport Flats Area (Columbia)
Catskill Creek in Catskill (Greene)
Dubois Creek into the RamsHorn
  Livingston Sanctuary (Greene)
RamsHorn Creek into the
  RamsHorn-Livingston Sanctuary
  (Greene)
Wallkill River National
  Wildlife Refuge (Sussex)

Moderate to Challenging

Wallkill River in Warwick
  (Orange)

Challenging

The Mouth of the Fishkill Creek
  in Beacon (Dutchess)
Tenmile River from Dover Plains
  to Webatuck (Dutchess)
Delaware River from Mongaup
  to Port Jervis (Orange)
Rondout Creek in the High Falls
  Area—Accord to High Falls
  (Ulster)
Stockport Creek to Claverack and
  Kinderhook Creeks (Columbia)

Most Challenging

Neversink River from
  Cuddebackville to Matamoras,
  PA (Orange)

Prologue

I grew up in a row house in Queens, in an area that was then a working-class neighborhood. Most of the dads commuted to their jobs in the city—a quarter-mile trek to the bus stop, a half-hour bus ride to Jamaica, and a forty-minute subway ride to Manhattan. The city was spreading out. In that time, way before anyone had coined the terms "sprawl" or "open space" or "forever wild," our houses boasted small backyards and smaller front ones, and the neighborhood had no parks. So, for us, the street was our playground. We played potsy and boxball on the sidewalks and punch ball, stoop ball, ringaleavio and hide-and-go-seek in the streets. The trees that a local builder with foresight had planted had not yet begun to die off; to our parents' chagrin their roots tore up our cesspools (the city had not yet installed sewers), and to our chagrin their roots tore up the sidewalks. We forever sported bloodied Band-Aids and cut-up knees, a consequence of roller skating and bicycling on the uneven pavement of those sidewalks. We hoped our Spaldings would not sail over the fence of our strange neighbor, my friend's Uncle Myron, who spent hours composting and planting, watering and grafting. He was an anomaly in our world of concrete, like the ragweed that would spring up in the cracks of the crumbling sidewalks. This is my earliest memory—and I only recognized it much later—of the competition and the conflict between the natural world and the man-made world. It was not until much later, too, that I realized the value of anomalies, of Uncle Myron, of the renegade weed that refused to be cemented over.

Now, as I take my boat out onto the creeks and rivers and ponds, I search for a wildness that no longer exists. Even in the most protected sanctuaries, an old Coke bottle lies partially hidden in the mud. Bending away from the road, the stream may leave the waterfront houses and their occupants with their barbecues and ATVs and plunge me into a magic world dripping with green. And then a jet plane passes overhead, a reminder of the constant intrusion of the world of man. I know that I will never see the same Hudson River that the Lenapes and the Wappingers and the early explorers saw three or four hundred years ago. The giant white pines are forever gone, cut down to make masts for a now defunct sailing industry. However, with our burgeoning awareness of the importance of the rivers, the swamps, the trees, the eagles, and the beavers, I am hopeful that we can live alongside what is left of these natural wonders and protect them. I am particularly hopeful as I remember the defiant weed growing between the cracks in the sidewalk in Queens.

Introduction

Fishing on the Susquehanna in July

I have never been fishing on the Susquehanna
or on any river for that matter
to be perfectly honest.

Not in July or any month
have I had the pleasure—if it is a pleasure—
of fishing on the Susquehanna.

I am more likely to be found
in a quiet room like this one—
a painting of a woman on the wall,

a bowl of tangerines on the table—
trying to manufacture the sensation
of fishing on the Susquehanna.

There is little doubt
that others have been fishing
on the Susquehanna,

rowing upstream in a wooden boat,
sliding the oars under the water
then raising them to drip in the light.

But the nearest I have ever come to
fishing on the Susquehanna
was one afternoon in a museum in Philadelphia

when I balanced a little egg of time
in front of a painting
in which that river curled around a bend

under a blue cloud-ruffled sky,
dense trees along the banks,
and a fellow with a red bandanna

sitting in a small, green
flat-bottom boat
holding the thin whip of a pole.

That is something I am unlikely
ever to do, I remember
saying to myself and the person next to me.

Then I blinked and moved on
to other American scenes
of haystacks, water whitening over rocks,

even one of a brown hare
who seemed so wired with alertness
I imagined him springing right out of the frame.

Billy Collins © 1998

There are not many things that I am unlikely ever to do.

Several years ago I was vacationing in the Outer Banks, where I have long been intrigued by the mixture of untamed wildlife and untamed beach. I'd spend hours reading the Carolina Coast or poring over the Outer Banks Vacation Guide, torn between the thrill of jet skiing, parasailing, surfing, and hang gliding and the peace of nature walks, sailing, dolphin watches, and kayaking. I'd lie on the beach—deserted by Jersey shore standards—planning out the week or two reprieve from my busy life of lesson plans and soccer games, grading papers and swim meets. The previous summer I'd rented jet skis and my younger daughter, Dara, young and full of mischief, veering left and accelerating at the same time, laughing, dumped me into the Pamlico Sound. On an earlier vacation, my older daughter Kendra and I had boarded a small, inflatable boat that Kitty Hawk Sports assured us was seaworthy, and, with a guide and a couple of other tourists, we dared the waves in search of a pod of dol-phins—which, incidentally, we found. The sports outfitters always do find them, I've been told, with the use of high tech equipment includ-ing helicopters, binoculars, and two-way radios. (Technology, too, has taken much of the uncertainty—and possibly the excitement—out of deep-sea fishing, another Outer Banks activity.) This year, armed with my North Carolina publications and my yellow highlighter, I targeted the yet untried sport of kayaking.

"Guess what?" I leaped up the steps to the deck of the house we'd rented.

My kids, seeing the paper, annotated and underscored, tucked under my arm, groaned. "What is it this time?"

"We're going kayaking."

The Outer Banks was my first experience with flatwater kayaking. We took four twelve-foot, one-person kayaks onto the sound and into the marshes and inlets teeming with herons and skimmers and egrets. And I was sold.

I'd made the decision to buy kayaks way back then on that first trip off the shore of Pea Island. I remember going into a store that sold small boats when I returned to New Paltz and the salesman asking me what kind of a kayak I wanted. I was taken aback, even more so when he tried to explain. "Are you going to do white water? Or do you want a sea kayak?"

Big purchases have always stopped me cold. Here the choices so over-whelmed me—there were sea kayaks and recreational kayaks, touring kayaks and ocean kayaks, sit-on-top kayaks and sporting kayaks—that I retreated into my landlubber world for close to a decade until Joe, my husband and best friend, asked, "Well, don't you want to buy kayaks? Let's go."

So we went.

Guided through the options by a helpful salesperson at a local sports outfitter, we buy two one-person Wilderness Systems Pungo 120 kayaks, intended for flat water—for quiet rivers, ponds, and creeks. Our second trip out, we pull our pickup truck over by the side of Route 299, a two-lane, high-speed thoroughfare not yet totally developed, yet each year looking more and more like Long Island, a strip that connects the New

Types of Kayaks

Arctic kayaks are the boats that all kayaks today are based on.

Folding kayaks are just as sturdy as regular kayak designs.

Inflatable kayaks: easy to use and light.

Kids' kayaks: Sit-on-top kids' kayaks are a good choice for most children.

Plastic kayaks are good for sturdy, affordable kayaks.

Sit-on-top kayaks are ideal for beginners.

Surf skis / Wave skis are small kayaks that are used for surfing the waves.

Wooden kayaks: Save money and look into building your own wooden kayaks.

Fiberglass kayaks are lighter and more versatile than other types of kayaks.

Recreational kayaks: There are so many different kinds of recreational kayaks that there is almost something for everybody.

Slalom kayaks are a form of whitewater racing kayak.

Solo versus tandem kayaks: Which are best for your trip? Solo or tandem kayaks?

Sprint kayaks are harder to keep upright than regular kayaks.

Squirt kayaks are designed to flip up on their ends to maneuver difficult rivers.

Surf kayaks are great for anybody who wants to try a new form of surfing.

Touring kayaks are sturdy enough to take on sea kayaking trips.

Whitewater racing kayaks are very maneuverable and can be used to do tricks.

Whitewater touring kayaks are the sturdiest kayaks for downriver travel.

Flatwater kayaks: Flatwater kayaking is easier to learn than any other type of kayaking.

River kayaks: River kayaking can entertain both beginners and experts.

Whitewater kayaks: Whitewater kayaking is an extreme form of kayaking.

Sea kayaks: Sea kayaking is the right activity for people who are looking for an adventure that is still fairly safe.

The prospective, first-time buyer confronts an overwhelming array of kayaks for sale, as suggested by this Internet listing (www. kayakhelp.com).

York State Thruway with the Mid-Hudson Bridge, and there we launch our boats onto the Black Creek.

The boats slip between the banks, overhanging branches stroking our arms. The creek turns one direction, then the other, and we leave behind both worries and the sounds of traffic—wheels spinning against the macadam, dull engine noise, an occasional horn. Hush! Our paddles break the surface of the water and shatter the peace as their unaccustomed motion startles a great blue heron that—Listen!—flying low above our heads, skitters through the air, large wings tearing leaves and twigs off trees, beating the wind.

Only a few miles and a few minutes from my home, I stumble on a bit of paradise. The stress and tension of work float downriver, and I emerge from my short evening boat trip calm and renewed. I turn to Joe and say, "You know, this hour and a half was a little vacation. These two boats have already paid for themselves."

New Paltz, at the foot of the Shawangunks, is a mecca to hikers and climbers. Over the next week I first search the local stores that cater to them, and then Barnes and Noble, for a book that tells about the ponds, lakes, rivers, and creeks that dot the area, a book that suggests magical places to put in a boat. It is when I realize that no such book exists that I resolve to attempt this guide.

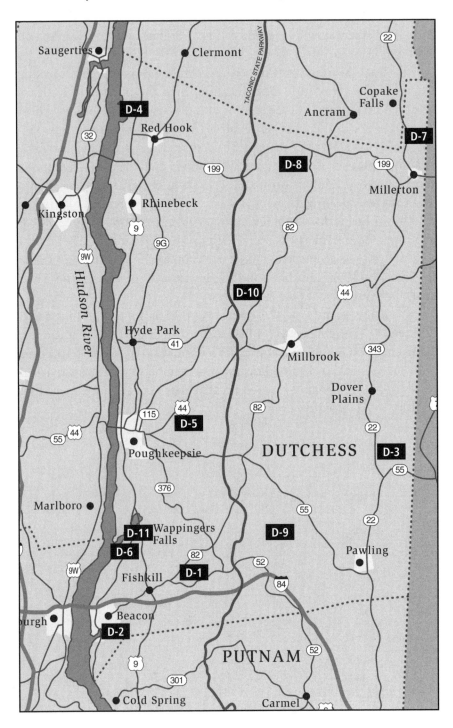

1

Dutchess County

I am with you, you men and women of a generation,
  or ever so many generations hence,
Just as you feel when you look on the river and sky, so I felt …
Just as you are refresh'd by the gladness of the river and
  the bright flow, I was refresh'd …

from "Crossing Brooklyn Ferry" by Walt Whitman

D-1 Fishkill Creek in Brinckerhoff
——Narrow and Shallow

- **Route:** Launch from the Doug Phillips Memorial Park on the north side of State Route 52 (SR-52) next to the Brinckerhoff. Head north as far as you can paddle. Turning back, pass your launch and go under SR-52, stopping before the top of a dam. Then return to the park.
- **Total Mileage:** Up to 4 miles round trip.
- **Difficulty:** Easy.
- **Setting:** Woods, fields, occasional houses.
- **Hazards:** A little over a quarter of a mile south of the launch are a dam and waterfall. You can approach them; they are clearly visible.
- **Remarks:** This portion of the Fishkill is navigable seasonally. North of the put-in, several riffles and shallows prevent further paddling. Even if you do portage beyond them, your progress will eventually be impeded by deadfall—several fallen trees totally block the creek.

The Fishkill Creek winds its way thirty-five miles through Dutchess County, emptying into the Hudson just south of Beacon. Although Holland colonized much of New York before the British settled here, little remains of the Dutch influence other than many place names. Fishkill was originally *Vis Kill*, the stream or *kill* aptly named for the abundance of fish or *vis*. As a humorous side note, a number of years ago some uninformed, though well-meaning, animal-protection advocates tried unsuccessfully to rename Fishkill, claiming that no right-minded people should name a town and a creek after cruelty to animals.

**Directions to Doug Phillips Memorial Park
from the Taconic State Parkway:**
Exit at SR-52 and go west. After 5 miles, you will go over Fishkill Creek. Doug Phillips Memorial Park is on your right. Pull in.

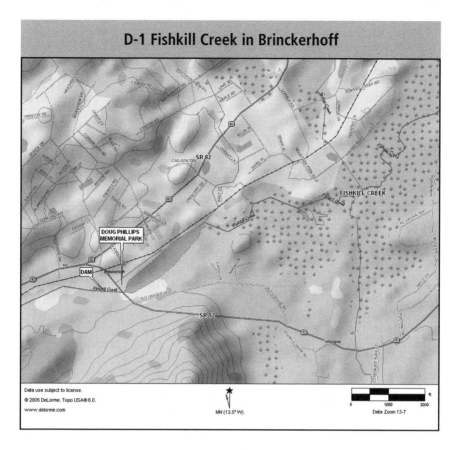

D-1 Fishkill Creek in Brinckerhoff

**Directions to Doug Phillips Memorial Park
from the New York State Thruway:**

Take exit 17 to SR-300 North. Turn right onto I-84 and follow it just under 8 miles, crossing over the Newburgh-Beacon Bridge and getting off at exit 12, SR-52 East. Continue on SR-52 for 3 miles; just after the intersection with SR-82, look for the park on your left.

The Paddle:

The best place for launching is behind the tennis courts. There it is easy to launch and easy to park your vehicle so that it will be visible from the creek when you return.

Turn upstream, to your left. At first you pass occasional houses on your left; the right bank is more desolate. The creek turns gently, but as

Perched on a fallen tree, a great blue heron—Fishkill Creek.

you go further you negotiate some serious switchbacks. You are liable to flush out some surprising—and surprised—wildlife as you round these bends. We pushed six or seven great blue herons upstream. They kept settling on the edge of the stream ahead, and after each of our turns these giant birds would take again to the sky. Once I turned around a bend just as a great horned owl swooped down and settled on some deadfall in my path, his back to me. He turned his head, saw me. I stopped paddling and remained still, trying not to scare him. The current drove me forward. As I came within feet of him, he took off, some prey I could not identify in his talons.

For the most part, the Fishkill Creek is both narrow—about thirty feet wide, occasionally narrower, occasionally wider—and shallow. These two physical features account for the difficulty in navigating much of the creek. Downed trees effectively block the entire waterway. Once down,

▶ **Fishkill Creek in Brinckerhoff**

they collect debris, forming dams and small pools of deeper water. Even a kayak will scrape bottom in many other spots. Just north of Doug Phillips Memorial Park, however, the creek is generally clear, providing a pretty place for a short paddle. Ultimately deadfall and shallow riffles will prevent you from going further. When you tire of power-paddling your kayak against the current through the riffles and of climbing over deadfall or around it, turn back.

If you continue a quarter of a mile past the park where you launched, you go under the SR-52 overpass and approach the top of a dam. At that point turn around and head back to your car.

D-2 The Mouth of the Fishkill Creek in Beacon
—A Marsh, a River, a Bay, and a Creek

■ **Route:** Starting in Riverfront Park in the city of Beacon, go south on the Hudson River for two miles, skirting Denning's Point. Go under the railroad trestle and explore the mouth of the Fishkill Creek.

■ **Total Mileage:** 5.5 miles round trip.

■ **Difficulty:** Challenging. **CH C** (See page 18.)

■ **Setting:** Open, wide river, often choppy; calm bay to the east of Denning's Point; marsh; woods and marshland adjacent to creek.

■ **Hazards:** Currents, tides, weather conditions, and boat traffic on the Hudson always pose some danger to small craft.

■ **Remarks:** Trip incorporates a great mix of open river, bay, marsh, and creek.

The place where the Fishkill Creek meets the Hudson River has been recognized as an especially scenic site with great wildlife viewing. Here Scenic Hudson, an environmental organization dedicated to the preservation and restoration of the Hudson River as a vital public resource, together with the city of Beacon, maintains the small 12-acre Madam Brett Park. Trails run through the park to observation decks overlooking the marsh at the mouth of the Fishkill. In this park, schoolchildren from the Beacon district study nature and the environment. A kayak offers a perfect way to visit the marsh, river, bay and creek—all rich in wildlife.

You can launch from Riverfront Park near the Metro-North train station in the city of Beacon. On weekends park for free on the street, in the park, or by the train station. On weekdays be sure to leave your car in the lot within the park itself. Launch from the southern tip of the park or from the public dock a hundred feet or so south of the park boundary.

Directions:
Take I-84 to Beacon, exit 11. Head south on State Route 9-D (SR-9D) and stay on it for a little over half a mile. Make a right onto Beekman Road. After the railroad, bear right onto Red Flynn Drive. This short road ends at the park.

▶ **The Mouth of the Fishkill Creek in Beacon**

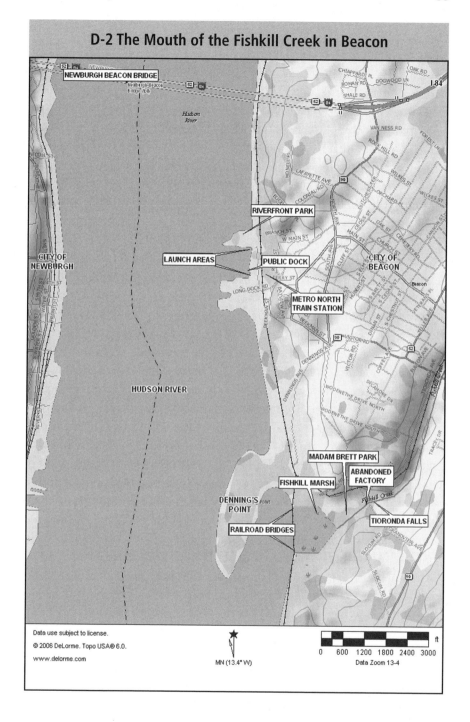

D-2 The Mouth of the Fishkill Creek in Beacon

NEWBURGH BEACON BRIDGE

Hudson River

I-84

RIVERFRONT PARK

CITY OF NEWBURGH

LAUNCH AREAS

PUBLIC DOCK

CITY OF BEACON

METRO NORTH TRAIN STATION

HUDSON RIVER

MADAM BRETT PARK

ABANDONED FACTORY

FISHKILL MARSH

DENNING'S POINT

TIORONDA FALLS

RAILROAD BRIDGES

Data use subject to license.
© 2006 DeLorme. Topo USA® 6.0.
www.delorme.com

MN (13.4° W)

0   600   1200 1800 2400 3000   ft
Data Zoom 13-4

The Paddle:

Since the dock area sits in a small, protected cove, you paddle straight out into the Hudson before turning left, southward. The river here is rather dramatic. Look north at the impressive double expanses of the Newburgh-Beacon Bridge as you paddle your way through the sailboats anchored near the park. Turn left toward Denning's Point, a peninsula that you will see jutting into the east side of the river. Though you remain far out of the principal shipping channel, crossing the bay creates the illusion of paddling in the middle of the river. Watch for boat traffic and be prepared for the wakes. If necessary turn your prow into the waves to avoid their hitting you broadside. To your right, in sharp contrast to the pristine state land on Denning's Point itself, is the city of Newburgh with its recently renovated riverfront, old factories and new housing.

It is over half a mile to the northern tip of Denning's Point and another half a mile until you round the bottom of the point. Once you clear the southern tip—during the summer months you will have to paddle further to avoid the water chestnuts that crowd the shoreline—you enter quieter water, an inlet protected by the peninsula. In the river itself cormorants—black, duck-like birds with orange beaks—perch on floating debris, seemingly unaffected by the jet skis, barges, and power boats, and Canadian geese honk, circle, and skitter over the surface. In the inlet shyer wildlife finds shelter, shielded from the winds and the wakes of boats. Here, look for the reticent herons and kingfishers. Around the edges, paddle through marsh with its dense underwater vegetation and its elaborate ecosystem. You see two sets of railroad bridges. Go under either one—the two will join eventually—and enter the mouth of Fishkill Creek. Poke around among the marsh plants and look at the low mountains rising in the distance. The observation deck on the left bank is part of the trail system traversing Madam Brett Park. As you continue upstream you begin to hear the unmistakable sounds of a waterfall. Another quarter of a mile or so and on your left you see the ruin of an old hat factory. Just ahead of you is an old bridge, and beyond that, Tioronda Falls.

The factory, the bridge and the falls in large part tell the story of Beacon. The Tioronda Hat Works, now empty, windows boarded up, suggests a bygone era when steam-powered ships chugged up and down the river, when hat factories employed hundreds, when all well-dressed

▶ **The Mouth of the Fishkill Creek in Beacon**

Sailboats at anchor in the Hudson near the Newburgh-Beacon Bridge.

people wore hats. It serves as a reminder of the decay of what was once a vibrant Hudson River community. At the same time, Tioronda Falls awakens us to the natural beauty of the area, the beauty that environmentalists like those in Scenic Hudson have sought actively to preserve in and around the city of Beacon. The city has invited discussion on what to do with the Tioronda Bridge, which has not yet been restored. Should it be reconstructed and widened? Should it be renovated as a pedestrian bridge?

Open discussion like this has revitalized Beacon during the last two decades. Thus the former city dump is now Riverfront Park, the park where you launched. Another abandoned factory has been transformed into Dia:Beacon, one of the largest contemporary art museums in the country. And an old paper clip factory on Denning's Point is slated to become a state-of-the-art research and education center studying rivers and estuaries.

Once you have reached the falls, you can go no further. Turn around and head back to Beacon's Riverfront Park. If you have time, combine your trip on the river with a visit to Dia:Beacon.

Helpful Web sites:

• http://www.cityofbeacon.org/Tour/TourBeaconsRenaissance.htm
  provides information on the recent changes in Beacon.

• http://www.clui.org/clui_4_1/lotl/v25/v25b.html
  likewise discusses the rebirth in Beacon with an emphasis
  on Dia:Beacon.

• http://www.nynjctbotany.org/lgtofc/beacontown.html
  lists important historic events concerning Beacon.

• http://www.diacenter.org/bindex.html
  the official Web site of Dia:Beacon, gives information on programs,
  events, directions, and hours.

A black-crowned night-heron stands amid water chestnuts in Fishkill Creek marsh.

▶ **The Mouth of the Fishkill Creek in Beacon**

Tenmile River from Dover Plains to Webatuck
—Fast and Fun

D-3

- ■ **Route:** Starting in Dover Plains, paddle south towards Wingdale. Follow the river as it turns east towards Connecticut, pulling out in Webatuck.
- ■ **Total Mileage:** 7.75 miles one way.
- ■ **Difficulty:** Challenging. **A R L D P O M** (See page 18.)
- ■ **Setting:** Rural landscape with hardwood forests, fields, farms, rolling hills.
- ■ **Hazards:** This is moving flat water. There are occasional shallow riffles with rocks and small rapids, some low hanging branches and deadfall. As with all moving water, caution must be taken.
- ■ **Remarks:** Requires two vehicles. Rainfall amounts will impact trip. Extremely low levels mean portages; high levels mean faster flow, necessitating greater care. Review "The Limitations of a Paddling Guide."

Ask Mid-Hudson whitewater enthusiasts to name some of the good, nearby places to canoe or kayak and they will mention the Esopus, the Delaware, and Tenmile River. I know the Delaware from my days just after college. A group of us would run Skinner Falls while the locals picnicked on the banks, gawking at the wild tourists dumped into the rock-strewn rapids and watching the canoes roll over. I know the Esopus from tubing the cold five-mile stretch out of Phoenicia with my kids on hot summer days. But until recently I had never heard of Tenmile River. It turns out that the river begins with the confluence of the Webatuck and Wassaic creeks, and then jogs and turns for seventeen miles—ten miles as the crow flies—through eastern Dutchess County, ending in the Housatonic River in Connecticut a little over half a mile from the state border. The course between Webatuck and the Housatonic is difficult, especially when water levels are high. But the section of the river between Dover Plains and Webatuck is moving flat water, interspersed with true flat water, riffles, and small rapids.

Since you can only paddle in one direction, this trip requires two vehicles. The take-out is in Webatuck before the serious rapids. Some paddlers park at Webatuck Craft Village, a collection of small stores adjacent to the river. But just west of there on the north side of State Route 55 (SR-55) are several pull-offs with river access.

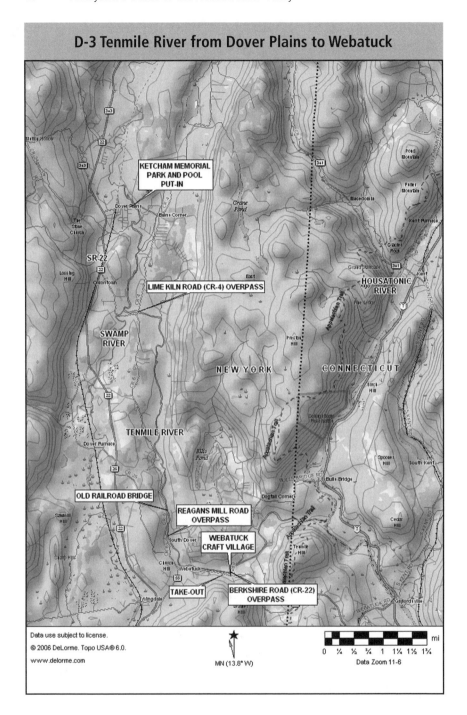

D-3 Tenmile River from Dover Plains to Webatuck

KETCHAM MEMORIAL PARK AND POOL PUT-IN

LIME KILN ROAD (CR-4) OVERPASS

SWAMP RIVER

HOUSATONIC RIVER

N E W   Y O R K   C O N N E C T I C U T

TENMILE RIVER

OLD RAILROAD BRIDGE

REAGANS MILL ROAD OVERPASS

WEBATUCK CRAFT VILLAGE

TAKE-OUT

BERKSHIRE ROAD (CR-22) OVERPASS

Data use subject to license.
© 2006 DeLorme. Topo USA® 6.0.
www.delorme.com
MN (13.8° W)

Data Zoom 11-6

▶ **Tenmile River from Dover Plains to Webatuck**

Directions to Webatuck:

Take I-84 to exit 20. (Or, take I-684 to where it ends.) Pick up SR-22 North. After 12 miles in Pawling, SR-22 and SR-55 join. When they split 7 miles ahead, bear right onto SR-55 East. Less than one mile further, SR-55 makes a hard right as it parallels the Tenmile River. In the next mile, before you reach Webatuck Craft Village, look for any of three pull-offs providing parking and fishing access to the water. Make sure that you will be able to both pull your boat up the bank and see your vehicle from the water.

Directions from Webatuck to
Ketcham Memorial Park in Dover Plains:

Take SR-55 West back to the intersection with SR-22. Turn right onto SR-22 North. At the light in the village of Dover Plains, turn right onto Mill Street. Mill Street crosses over the Tenmile River. Just before the bridge, turn right into Ketcham Memorial Park, the location of the town pool.

The Paddle:

The park does not have an actual boat access. The bank is somewhat steep and the water is moving, so the launch is not easy. Once in, you move quickly south, leaving the village behind. You would never guess that this stretch of river between Dover Plains and the first overpass does not veer more than a few hundred feet from Lime Kiln Road; the sounds of the moving water mask any road noise. Any houses along the Tenmile here must be set back, with the rising banks blocking them from view. The river alternates between flat water and gently moving water, offering a bit of excitement as the current rounds a bend, tending to push the kayak towards the shore on the outside of the curve. Two miles from Ketcham Park, the Swamp River, the northern flow of the Great Swamp, empties into Tenmile River. Just ahead you see the first of three overpasses as Lime Kiln Road crosses the river. The next two and a half miles—from the Lime Kiln overpass to where CR-6 approaches and then runs beside the river—are amazing.

Right after the bridge, the current, now stronger, drove my kayak into a fallen tree that effectively blocked the river and pinned me there. While Joe, benefiting from my paddling ahead and his observations of my predicament, deftly turned to the left shore and portaged around the obstacle, I spent the next ten minutes climbing onto the massive twin trunks of the tree and dragging my kayak up onto the tree trunks and over them. Wet from the water and sweaty from the exertion, I got back into the kayak and met up with Joe, who was calmly waiting up ahead. We continued down the river. On our left the landscape, now opening up, revealed low mountains rising dramatically. Farms with trim barns and buildings and manicured fields rolled towards the banks. Five or ten minutes further, the woods once again closed in, trees and vegetation obscuring all signs of civilization. In this portion of the river, there were more rapids and they were more challenging. We had to remain alert, avoiding rocks jutting out and those hidden just beneath the surface. On occasion, the fronts of our boats dipped and water sloshed in, wetting our clothes. Though a little soggy, we managed the river easily and were exhilarated by both the picturesque scenery and the joy of the challenge.

The landscape along Tenmile River suddenly opens up.

▶ Tenmile River from Dover Plains to Webatuck

As you paddle the final section, you hear road noise and again see occasional houses as Old Post Road now runs right next to the river. It is still pretty and, despite the houses, surprisingly clean. The river is straighter now; the twists that characterized the beginning section, the bends that the current made a bit difficult to negotiate, have all but disappeared. A little over a mile later you paddle under an old railroad bridge. In another half a mile you approach the Reagans Mill Road overpass. A bit further and the Tenmile River turns eastward, beginning its final journey to the Housatonic in Connecticut. Keep an eye out now for your vehicle. The take-out may not be easy—you must deal with both a steep bank and moving water—so take care.

D-4 Tivoli Bays in Red Hook
—Twin Beauties

- **Route:** Beginning at the boat launch provided by the Hudson River National Estuarine Research Reserve in North Bay, explore several channels before entering the Hudson River near Magdalen Island. Go south. Below Cruger Island, go under the railroad bridge, entering South Bay. Cross the bay to the mouth of the Saw Kill before heading back.
- **Total Mileage:** About 7 miles round trip.
- **Difficulty:** Moderate. **A** (or **CH C**) (See page 18.)
- **Setting:** Freshwater tidal marsh, open river, and shallow cove.
- **Hazards:** Currents, tides, weather conditions, and boat traffic on the Hudson always pose some danger to small craft. Tidal considerations: during low tide, the water recedes dramatically and some of the channels become impassable; at high tide the water level approaches the bottom of some of the railroad bridges leading into the bay.
- **Remarks:** The channels create a kind of maze within North Bay and can be confusing. Low tide makes many of the channels in North Bay inaccessible and exposes mudflats in South Bay. In summer the growth of water chestnuts makes it difficult to negotiate South Bay.

Tivoli Bays offers a unique opportunity to explore freshwater tidal marshes in an area maintained jointly by the New York State DEC and the Hudson River National Estuarine Research Reserve. The Department of Environmental Conservation has designated it a wildlife management area, providing sanctuary to a slew of species, while the Reserve uses it as a laboratory for monitoring and understanding the function of the river and its adjacent marshes and bays.

Directions from the Thruway:
From the New York State Thruway, take the Kingston exit (19), then State Route 28 (SR-28) West for about a quarter of a mile, turning right onto US-209 North (which becomes SR-199) towards the Kingston-Rhinecliff Bridge. After you have crossed the bridge over the Hudson (about 5 miles), make your first left onto County Route 103 (CR-103). This scenic route passes the Poets' Walk Romantic Landscape Park, a pretty area with maintained hiking trails from the bluff down to the river. After less than

D-4 Tivoli Bays in Red Hook

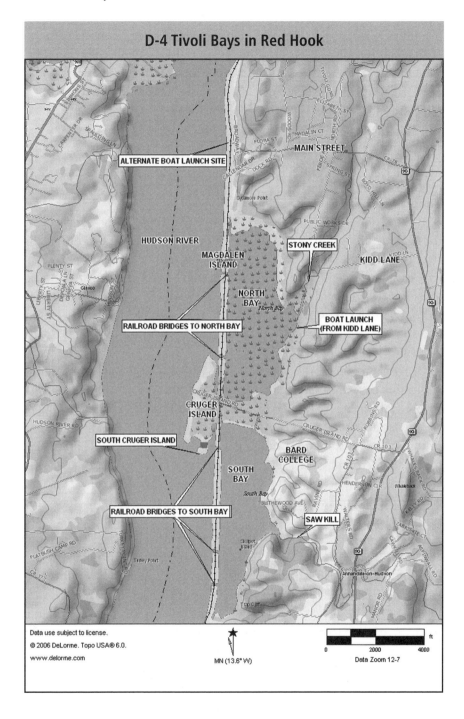

Data use subject to license.
© 2006 DeLorme. Topo USA® 6.0.
www.delorme.com

MN (13.6° W)

0   2000   4000   ft

Data Zoom 12-7

five miles, CR-103 will wind through the Bard College campus before it ends at SR-9G. Make a left, heading north towards Tivoli. Stay on SR-9G for 1.5 miles. Turn left onto Kidd Lane, which leads to the boat launch.

Directions from the Taconic State Parkway:

Exit the Taconic State Parkway at SR-199. Go west on SR-199 for a little over 9 miles. Turn right onto SR-9G, following it north for 3.5 miles. Turn left onto Kidd Lane.

The Paddle:

A warning about the launch: it is not an easy access. You can drive past the parking area to load and unload, but from there the descent to the river is difficult. You walk down a steep path, but this does not take you to the water. You still have to go down a stairway to get to the dock. And after you have taken your boats down to the dock, you have to go back to your vehicle, move it to the parking area and hike down again. Now you can launch your canoes or kayaks into the mouth of Stony Creek. North Bay lies to your left.

There is an alternative access to the North Bay. If you are comfortable navigating on the Hudson, you can put in from a beach in the village of Tivoli. Continue on SR-9G past Kidd Road a little over a half a mile to the intersection with Broadway (CR-78). Turn left onto Broadway and go towards the Hudson and through the center of Tivoli. Take Diana Street to the end across the tracks, unload, park and launch. Keeping near the shore, paddle to your left. If you stay between Magdalen Island and the eastern bank, you will see the railroad bridge to your left. Under the bridge is North Bay.

On my most recent visit to North Bay, my husband and I began our trip from inside the bay at the DEC launch, armed with an HRNERR brochure with its official map of the region showing the established creeks and channels. We headed left, south, away from the mouth of Stony Creek and circled a small island of cattails and other water plants. We came to a fork. The right branch went on towards channels leading to the Hudson River under the northernmost rail bridge across from Magdalen Island. On the map, the left fork appeared as an irregular splotch, like a hand with fingers reaching into the marsh. Wanting to explore, and intrigued by its very shape on the map, we turned left.

▶ **Tivoli Bays in Red Hook**

Marsh grasses border winding channels in North Bay.

I quietly paddled ahead, watching for wildlife, though seeing little in the hot mid-afternoon, turning now and then into dead-end passages, tentacles reaching into the marsh. Looking for Joe, I returned, called for him, and thought I heard his answer in the distance. I paddled in his direction, but walled in as I was by tall grasses, I could not find him and could no longer hear him. Figuring that we would meet up by the rail bridge—since we had planned to go into the Hudson and make our way to South Bay—I looked for the current. No problem. The water was gushing into the bay with about two hours until high tide. I simply paddled against the current. The view suddenly opened up and I got my bearings with the help of familiar mountains and the electric poles running alongside the railroad tracks. Pushing south, I found myself approaching the southern railroad bridge leading out into the Hudson by the tip of Cruger Island. According to the official map, there was no way to get from the boat launch to where I was. Such is the effect of tides. I glided easily over pools that would disappear as the tide went out. And I waited, hoping Joe would find his way through that maze of channels, but doubting he would.

When my phone rang, I remembered that fortunately we both were carrying cell phones, those symbols of modern technology that we loved and hated, blessed and cursed.

"Where *are* you?" we both asked at the same time.

We reconnected in the Hudson. Joe paddled down from the rail bridge by Magdalen Island. I hunkered down and scooted under the bridge by Cruger Island—almost impassable as the tide rose.

From North Bay, paddle south on the west side of Cruger Island, which, despite its name, looks like a peninsula jutting into river. Rounding the tip, turn towards the shore, staying to the east of South Cruger Island. There, right next to the island, is the northernmost rail bridge signaling the first of three openings into South Bay.

Having grown up on Long Island, I have a definite concept of what a bay should look like. Say "bay" and I think Jamaica Bay or Zachs Bay, an open expanse of saltwater partially protected by land. While neither North nor South Bay is saltwater—north of Poughkeepsie, despite the tides, the Hudson is freshwater—during high tide South Bay, with its 275 acres of open water partially fringed by forest, looks like a bay. In most of North Bay, on the other hand, you cannot make out the shore opposite; you can only see the narrow channels winding through the fields of cattails and perhaps gain a glimpse of the hills in the distance. Floating everywhere during our late-May trip, the spiked seeds of the invasive water chestnuts bobbed in the churning water of South Bay. We had seen none in North Bay. The difference between the two bays is staggering.

The partially hidden Bard College overlooks the eastern shore of South Bay. On the edge of the campus, the Saw Kill, making its way to the Hudson, flows into the bay. Paddle across the cove to investigate. An elevation change and the resulting waterfall at the mouth of the Saw Kill prevent any further exploration of the creek. The outgoing tide rushing under the three bridges signals that it is time to head back.

Late that afternoon, rather spent and not so quiet, we made our way back up the Hudson. Passing a large rock protruding out of the water, we alarmed four large snapping turtles that one by one scuttled into the

▶ **Tivoli Bays in Red Hook**

water, splashing our kayaks. Moments later I looked up. Directly above us a bald eagle perched in a tree.

I led Joe back the way I had come. We had only a few minutes left, for with the water now rushing out of the bays under the bridges, the tidal pools we crossed were very shallow. I paddled past the boat launch to poke around in the mouth of Stony Creek, a beautiful spot with clear water and dense foliage. The trunk of a huge fallen tree blocked any further progress up the creek.

D-5 | Wappinger Creek from Pleasant Valley to Poughkeepsie
—Moving Flat Water and Flushing Geese

- **Route:** Launch at Pleasant Valley Recreation Park and paddle south with the current. Take-out is at Greenvale Park in the Town of Poughkeepsie just north of Red Oaks Mill.
- **Total Mileage:** 6.8 miles one way.
- **Difficulty:** Moderate. **R L P O M** (See page 18.)
- **Setting:** Mostly forested, occasional houses generally set back from creek.
- **Hazards:** This is moving flat water. There are occasional shallow riffles with rocks, small rapids, and some low-hanging branches. As with all moving water, caution must be taken.
- **Remarks:** Requires two vehicles. When water levels are normal, entire section can be run. When water levels are low, some portages are necessary. Review "The Limitations of a Paddling Guide."

Wappinger Creek runs southwestward from its headwaters at Thompson Pond at the foot of Stissing Mountain in Pine Plains to meet the Hudson in the hamlet of New Hamburg. The northernmost part runs through wetlands and woodlands as a narrow stream. About a mile south of Salt Point it joins up with Little Wappinger Creek and shortly after widens into a principal watercourse contiguous to the densely populated Poughkeepsie-Wappingers Falls area. Considering the density of the population near the creek, the land through which it runs is surprisingly undeveloped and clean. As with most of the creeks in the Hudson River Valley, the original flow of the stream has been unalterably changed by the construction of dams, and true flat water sections alternate with riffles and small rapids. The section from Pleasant Valley to Greenvale Park in the Town of Poughkeepsie offers an almost seven-mile course of "moving flat water."

Directions to Greenvale Park from the Mid-Hudson Bridge:
Stay on Route 44-55 for 2 miles to Raymond Avenue. Make a right. Raymond Avenue ends in one mile at New Hackensack Road, also called State Route 376 (SR-376). Turn left and continue on New Hackensack Road for 1.25 miles. Turn left onto Greenvale Farms Road and into the park.

▶ **Wappinger Creek from Pleasant Valley to Poughkeepsie**

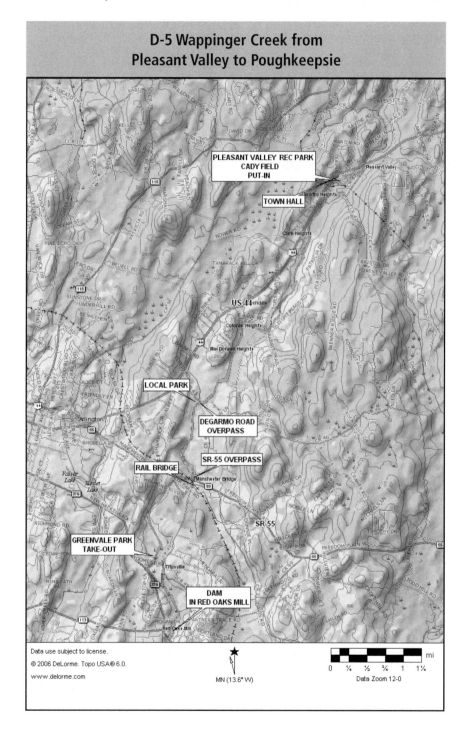

D-5 Wappinger Creek from Pleasant Valley to Poughkeepsie

PLEASANT VALLEY REC PARK
CADY FIELD
PUT-IN

TOWN HALL

US 44

LOCAL PARK

DEGARMO ROAD
OVERPASS

SR-55 OVERPASS

RAIL BRIDGE

GREENVALE PARK
TAKE-OUT

SR-55

DAM
IN RED OAKS MILL

Data use subject to license.

© 2006 DeLorme. Topo USA® 6.0.

www.delorme.com

MN (13.6° W)

0   ¼   ½   ¾   1   1¼   mi

Data Zoom 12-0

Directions to Greenvale Park from the Taconic State Parkway:
Exit the Taconic at SR-55. Go west toward Poughkeepsie for 2.5 miles. At fork turn left onto County Route 49 (CR-49), also called Titusville Road. Stay on CR-49 for just under 2 miles. Turn left onto CR-44 (Red Oaks Mill Road), which ends in less than a mile. Make a sharp right onto SR-376 (New Hackensack Road). Turn right onto Greenvale Farms Road 1.2 miles ahead.

Directions from Greenvale Park to Pleasant Valley Recreation Park:
Make a right out of the park onto New Hackensack Road. Go 1.25 miles. At fork with Hooker Avenue, take Raymond Avenue towards the right. Go 1 mile, then turn right onto Route 44-55. In a quarter of a mile, the routes split. Stay left, following US-44 for 5 miles into Pleasant Valley. Look for the town hall on your right. The park is directly behind the town hall.

The Paddle:
Launch your boat at Pleasant Valley Rec Park behind the soccer fields. Put in carefully—the water is moving. The contrast between the busy roads you just left, with their strip malls and traffic, is striking. Though the creek runs just east of Poughkeepsie, with a population of roughly 30,000 people, once in the water you feel that you are indeed in the country. You wind your way through woods and occasional backyards, most of the houses tastefully set back. I was struck by how relatively litter-free the creek was for a waterway that is not designated a protected area. Between Pleasant Valley and Greenvale Park only two roads cross the creek, and none for the first four miles. The first overpass is Degarmo Road, a route connecting State Routes 44 and 55 a little over a mile after they split as they head east out of Poughkeepsie. As we paddled down this part of the creek, only a golf course and occasional parks indicated that we were, at most, two or three miles from a city. A little more than a mile further we passed first under SR-55, and immediately after that under a railroad bridge.

Like so many of our railways, this one is no longer used. This stretch of abandoned railway goes east to Hopewell Junction in Dutchess County, where it ends abruptly—Metro-North still uses the track south of that point. To the west it traverses Poughkeepsie, crosses the old railroad bridge just north of the Mid-Hudson Bridge, then meanders through Ulster and Orange counties. I reflect for a moment on the tremendous effort that went into the construction of the railroads that crisscross our

▶ **Wappinger Creek from Pleasant Valley to Poughkeepsie**

country. I ponder the decisions that were made to expand our system of roads, highways, and interstates—to support the trucking industry and give up on the railways. I wonder what impact a national mass transportation system might have had on pollution, fuel consumption, and congestion. I think of the abandoned rail lines all across our country and the enormous waste.

Kayaking on moving water is a different experience than kayaking on flat water. Nature still surrounds you—the water still supports you, and the trees on the banks still cradle you. Yet the pace is not so leisurely. Paddling now required our full attention. There were rocks to avoid, low limbs to duck, shallows to circumvent. I tucked my camera into a waterproof case. Driven forward by the current, we flushed out mallards and geese and pushed them ahead. And then, when we reached a section of quiet water, we would slow down, look around, see the beauty around us.

Important: watch for Greenvale Park on your right about a mile and a half past the railroad bridge. You do not want to miss it. Not too far beyond is Red Oaks Mill, where the creek waters hurtle over its dam.

Parent geese urge their babies onto the shore of Wappinger Creek and away from our kayaks.

D-6 | **The Mouth of the Wappinger Creek in Wappingers Falls** *—From the Creamery to the Hudson*

■ **Route:** From the Hudson Greenway launch area, paddle southwest a mile and a half through the Wappinger Creek and into the Hudson River. On the return trip, pass the launch area and go past the Market Street Industrial Park to the foot of the falls.

■ **Total Mileage:** 4–5 miles round trip.

■ **Difficulty: Easy to moderate.** (If you go into the Hudson, **CH C.** See page 18.)

■ **Setting:** As you head toward the Hudson River, freshwater marsh backs up to mixed woodland. On the east bank, occasional houses; the steep west bank has prevented development. In the other direction the woods give way as you approach the historical commercial area of New Hamburg.

■ **Hazards:** If you choose to paddle in the Hudson River, remember that currents, tides, weather conditions, and boat traffic on the Hudson always pose some danger to small craft.

■ **Remarks:** During the summer months water chestnuts choke up a good portion of this part of the Wappinger Creek. However, a deeper channel in the middle does allow paddling.

Wappinger Creek flows into the Hudson River in the small hamlet of New Hamburg. The hamlet itself and the mouth of the creek offer a quiet respite from the busy US-9 corridor of mega-shopping centers and strip malls that runs between Poughkeepsie and Wappingers Falls. On the creek, the bustle of the Dutchess County urban areas seems much farther away than a mere mile or two.

Directions:

The Reese Park launch area, designated by the Hudson River Greenway Water Trail as an official launch site, has parking and an easy access to the creek. To get there from I-84, take exit 11 just east of the Newburgh-Beacon Bridge and get onto State Route 9-D (SR-9D) North. In 5 miles turn left onto County Route 28 (CR-28), also called New Hamburg Road. Stay on CR-28 for just under a mile. Before the creek, turn right onto Creek Road. Just over a mile you will see the entrance to Reese Park on your right. Pass it. On your left is a parking area and ramp down to the creek.

▶ **The Mouth of the Wappinger Creek in Wappingers Falls**

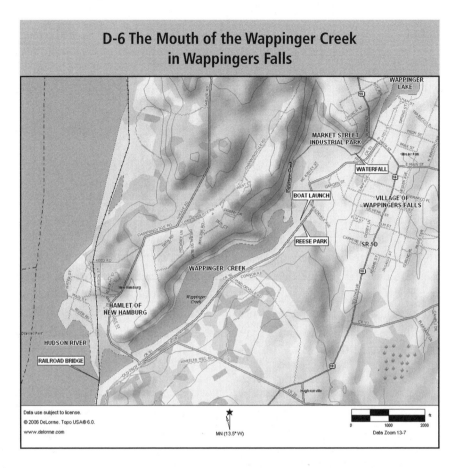

D-6 The Mouth of the Wappinger Creek in Wappingers Falls

The Paddle:

This particular access offers a unique perspective on this portion of Wappinger Creek. Turn left towards the Hudson and face an outstanding area for wildlife viewing. Turn right and gaze into a bit of regional history.

Always drawn by the appeal of the Hudson River, I chose the southern route first and turned my kayak left toward the actual mouth of the creek. First I made my way through a narrow opening in the water chestnuts, a path seemingly made by the small boats using this launch, and paddled out to the deeper water of the middle of the creek, which is wide enough here to accommodate the schooners and steamers that once sailed and chugged their way to the commercial center of Wappingers Falls. The right bank is rather steep, its very steepness having protected it over the decades from development. The left bank is level. This feature allowed for the construction of Creek Road, which, as its name suggests, parallels the creek, and allowed also for building the occasional houses seen from the water. Water chestnuts are the predominant plant in these marshes adjacent to the creek. They are thick and invasive and tend to take over entire marsh areas, though in places some native species still hold on fighting for their existence. Among the plants in the shallows, I scared up some great blue herons and a smaller green heron. The birds flew fifty, a hundred feet ahead and settled again amid the water chestnuts.

I continued on and after a mile or so paddled under the New Hamburg Road overpass. Two men standing on the bridge pulled in lines they had dropped into the water and raised traps. "What for?" I called and one of them answered, "Crabs. But tiny. Way too small." Up ahead was the railroad bridge demarking the line between river and creek. I paddled underneath and the Hudson River opened before me—across the river, Ulster County to the north, Orange County, and the Hudson Highlands; on this side of the river, the New Hamburg marina—all seen through the latticework of old pier stanchions, remnants of a bygone

Looking southward down the Hudson from the mouth of Wappinger Creek.

▶ The Mouth of the Wappinger Creek in Wappingers Falls

era, stanchions that guided ships in the nineteenth and early twentieth centuries into the creek to load and unload at the harbor in Wappingers Falls. The river was fairly calm with little boat traffic, and I explored a bit before heading back.

On my way back, I passed the Reese Park boat launch and continued upstream towards what used to be the commercial center of Wappingers Falls. Around a bend, and suddenly I was confronted by the history of the place. As I paddled forward, old factory buildings—many clearly renovated—loomed up on both sides of the creek. Here, at the foot of the waterfall that gave the town its name, eighteenth-century industrialists erected factories that could use both the power generated by the falls and the water route up the creek from the Hudson. At first this complex was the Garner Print Works, a plant that printed on and dyed fabric. In the very early twentieth century the factory was sold and reopened as the Dutchess Bleachery, which at its height employed 1,150 to 1,200 people. It gained fame, for in the early 1920s, at a time when relations between most factory owners and workers could be described as hostile at best, the company introduced the novel idea of shared management with the workers. Eventually, in 1954, the Dutchess Bleachery shut its doors. For the next fifty years most of this commercial area remained neglected and most of the buildings remained vacant. Recently, some far-sighted planners have tried to give new life to the site, enticing businesses to renovate and move in and urging the state to clean up some toxic waste that leaches into the ground and the creek. I paddled past new and hopeful signs renaming this "The Market Street Industrial Park."

The sound of the waterfall urged me forward and I paddled right up to the foot of the falls before I turned around and proceeded back to my car.

D-7–D-11 Dutchess County Ponds and Lakes

D-7 Rudd Pond in Millerton (Taconic State Park)

■ **How to get there:** Exit the Taconic State Parkway at State Route 199 (SR-199). Go east on SR-199 until it ends in 15 miles. Turn left onto US-44. In 2 miles, in Millerton, make a left onto County Route 62 (Rudd Pond Road). The entrance to Taconic State Park is 2.2 miles on your right.

■ **Where to put in:** You can put in right next to the park office or anywhere along the eastern side of the lake, which is gently sloped, allowing for easy access.

■ **Remarks:** The northern edge of the 56-acre lake is marsh. The other sides are woods and grass. Though the area is not developed, the road adjacent to the park is visible from the lake. Situated in the northeastern corner of Dutchess County, the lake is in Taconic State Park. Daily admission fees are charged per car. The annual Empire Pass may be purchased, which gives access to all New York State parks. To use your own boat, you must purchase the New York State Taconic Region annual boat pass.

Web sites:

• http://nysparks.state.ny.us/parks/info.asp?parkID=132 gives information about the use of the park.

• http://www.dec.state.ny.us/website/dfwmr/fish/lakemaps/ruddpd-map.pdf offers a map of Rudd Pond. Though not meant for navigational use, this map gives water surface area, depths, contours, and species of fish found.

D-8 Stissing Pond in Pine Plains

■ **How to get there:** Take the Taconic State Parkway to State Route 199 (SR-199). Stay on SR-199 East 6 miles. Turn right onto Lake Road, which circles Stissing Pond.

■ **Where to put in:** There are two places where you can park your car and launch your kayak. You can turn left onto Beach Road. On your right, on the northeastern edge of the pond before you get to the town

▶ **Dutchess County Ponds and Lakes**

beach, is a parking area and boat access maintained for the public by the Pine Plains Lions Club. Or, you can continue on Lake Drive towards the southeast corner of the pond, where pull-offs on both sides of the road can accommodate four to five cars.

■ **Remarks:** Pine Plains has three good fishing lakes—Stissing Pond, Thompson Pond, and Twin Island Lake. Thompson Pond, the headwaters of Wappinger Creek, is part of a nature preserve maintained by the Nature Conservancy, which offers hiking and bird watching, but no boating. Twin Island Lake has no easy public access. However, Stissing Pond is both beautiful and accessible. This is a 150-acre glacial lake with clear water against a backdrop of low mountains. From the lake you see the 1,403-foot Stissing Mountain with its observation tower. The lake's uneven and jagged shoreline includes some forest as well as some marsh. Despite some development along the shore, the pond remains relatively wild, natural and pristine.

Web site:

• http://www.dec.state.ny.us/website/dfwmr/fish/lakemaps/stispd-map.pdf offers a map of Stissing Pond. Though not meant for navigational use, the map gives water surface area, depths, contours, and species of fish found.

D-9 Sylvan Lake in Beekman

■ **How to get there:**
From the New York State Thruway: Take exit 17, Newburgh. Bear right after the toll booths onto State Route 300 (Union Avenue) for a half mile. Take I-84 East for 16 miles to the Taconic State Parkway (exit 16N). Stay on the Taconic for 7 miles.
From the Taconic State Parkway: Exit onto County Route 82 (CR-82) heading northeast. After less than a quarter of a mile, turn right onto CR-10 (Sylvan Lake Road). In about 2 miles you will see the lake on your right. Look for a small public pull-off on your right.

■ **Where to put in:** The small unpaved parking area on the right of Sylvan Lake Road is adjacent to the lake.

■ **Remarks:** The 115-acre lake is situated in a town with a suburban feel. Houses, a camp, and resorts dot the sides of the lake.

Web site:

• http://www.dec.state.ny.us/website/dfwmr/fish/lakemaps/sylvnlkmap. pdf offers a map of Sylvan Lake. Though not meant for navigational use, the map gives water surface area, depths, contours, and species of fish found.

D-10 Upton Lake in Stanford

■ **How to get there:** Take the Taconic State Parkway to Salt Point Turnpike exit. Go northeast on Salt Point Turnpike for a little over a mile and a half. Turn right onto Grove Way. Make an immediate left onto Anderson Road.

■ **Where to put in:** On the right of Anderson Road is a parking area. The sign there indicates directions to the right-of-way to the lake. The walk down to the lake is gentle, but you will need to carry your boat the two or three hundred yards to the launch.

■ **Remarks:** No powered boats of any sort are permitted on the 44-acre lake. Most of it is private and the use of the lake, which is surrounded by houses, mostly summer homes, is controlled by the homeowners association. A sign states that public access to this small lake is provided courtesy of the Federation of Dutchess County Fish and Game Clubs. Signs on houses, streets, and homes, all less welcoming, indicate that the area is restricted and proclaim loudly, "No Trespassing."

Web site:

• http://www.dec.state.ny.us/website/dfwmr/fish/lakemaps/uptolkmap. pdf offers a map of Upton Lake. Though not meant for navigational use, the map gives water surface area, depths, contours, and species of fish found.

▶ **Dutchess County Ponds and Lakes**

D-11 Wappinger Lake in Wappingers Falls

■ **How to get there:**

From the New York State Thruway: Take exit 17, bearing right on exit ramp onto State Route 300 (SR-300) North, also called Union Ave. After half a mile turn right onto I-84 East for 4.8 miles.

From I-84: Get off at exit 11 and head north on SR-9D (SR-52). Continue on SR-9D into the village of Wappingers Falls, about 6.6 miles. Turn right onto Spring Street, which ends at the lake in less than .25 mile.

■ **Where to put in:** There is parking, a public launch, and a ramp.

■ **Remarks:** The 88-acre lake is visible from US-9, which crosses it via an overpass. The incongruity of the natural environment, though marred by refuse, and the busy thoroughfare typifying American development gone berserk with its box stores, mega-malls and fast-food eateries, is striking. The southwest outlet of the lake, which leads to the Hudson, is blocked by a dam. You can paddle northward about half a mile into a quite beautiful area where the sounds of a waterfall (which ultimately prevents you from going any further) drowns out the sounds of the car engines.

Web site:

• http://www.dec.state.ny.us/website/dfwmr/fish/lakemaps/wapplkmap. pdf offers a map of Wappinger Lake. Though not meant for navigational use, the map gives water surface area, depths, contours, and species of fish found.

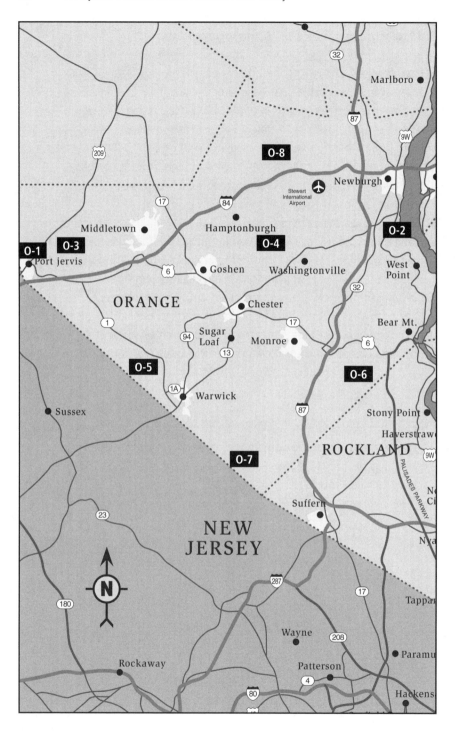

2

Orange County

What would the world be, once bereft

Of wet and wildness? Let them be left,

O let them be left, wildness and wet;

Long live the weeds and the wilderness yet.

from "Inversnaid" by Gerard Manley Hopkins

0-1 Delaware River from Mongaup to Port Jervis
—Beyond Flat Water

- **Route:** From the Mongaup put-in, paddle downriver along the Pennsylvania border with Orange County. Get out at West End Beach In Port Jervis.
- **Total Mileage:** 6 miles one way.
- **Difficulty:** Challenging. **O M W** (See page 18.)
- **Setting:** This southern portion of the Upper Delaware River flows through a gorge marked by deep cliffs and forest before it reaches a populated area with Matamoras to the west and Port Jervis to the east.
- **Hazards:** Rocks. Class I rapids. (On international class I-VI scale, class I are the easiest. Class I—moving water with few riffles and small waves. Few or no obstructions. Class II—easy rapids with waves up to three feet and wide clear channels that are obvious. This, according to the American Canoe Association.)
- **Remarks:** Requires two vehicles. This trip combines flat water, moving flat water, and white water. The water, even in summertime, is often cold. In a kayak you will get wet. Because of reservoir releases, there is always sufficient water to kayak, but levels vary. In late summer and periods of drought, rapids will be tamer and rocks will be more evident.

Although by no means flat water, the Delaware River, so famous for water recreation, begs for inclusion in any local book on kayaking. In its northern section the river marks the state boundary between New York and Pennsylvania. Below Port Jervis it separates Pennsylvania from New Jersey. The 330-mile-long Delaware is utterly different from the 315-mile-long Hudson, which runs roughly parallel to it. Between Albany and New York City, the Hudson River is wide enough, and today deep enough, to accommodate ocean vessels. The average depth of the Delaware, on the other hand, is four to five feet—though it boasts many deeper holes, the deepest of which, at Narrowsburg, is 113 feet. The Hudson registers 6.8 feet above sea level at the port of Albany and 6.6 feet above sea level at the lower tip of Manhattan. This absence of elevation change allows ocean tides to control the current. Not so for the Delaware. The Delaware's average descent of six feet every mile, coupled

▶ **Delaware River from Mongaup to Port Jervis**

O-1 Delaware River from Mongaup to Port Jervis

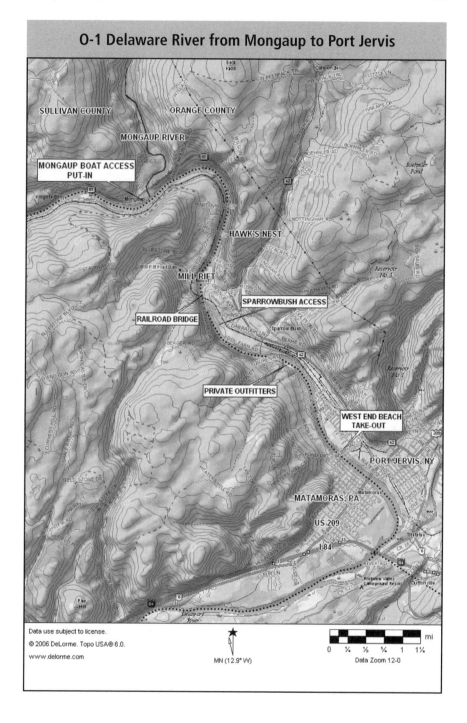

with its narrower course and its shallower bottom, accounts for its down-stream current and rapids that outdoor adventurer-seekers love.

A seventy-three-mile section of the river between Hancock, New York, and Mill Rift, Pennsylvania, has been designated a part of the National Wild and Scenic River System. In this section alone, the Pennsylvania Fish and Boat Commission and the New York State Department of Environmental Conservation and other town and state agencies maintain over twenty boat and fishing access points. While private ownership of land limits the use of many other waterways, all levels of government have joined to encourage public use of the Delaware.

Directions to West End Beach:

To paddle the river as it abuts Orange County, leave one vehicle at your end point—West End Beach in Port Jervis. To get there, get off I-84 at exit 1 and get onto US-6 West. Stay on US-6 for 2.4 miles as it heads first north and then turns southwest. Just before the bridge to Pennsylvania, turn right onto Water Street. In three blocks, Water Street will jog slightly and change its name to River Road. Follow River Road for less than half a mile to Ferry Street. The city beach with parking is to your left.

Directions to the Mongaup launch:

To get to the launch site, leave the beach by turning left onto West Main Street. In a little under a mile, West Main ends. Bear left onto Sleepy Hollow Road, which intersects with State Route 97 (SR-97) in less than a mile. Turn left onto SR-97, the scenic road that follows the course of the river. In four miles you cross into Sullivan County (the Mongaup River divides Orange and Sullivan). Turn immediately into the Mongaup Valley Wildlife Area, a river access maintained by the New York State DEC.

The Paddle:

Before you launch, make sure to secure in plastic any items that should not get wet—cell phone, camera, remote car keys—and fasten your life jacket snugly. The river where you put in is moving rather quickly, and the first rapids you encounter—most likely caused by the Mongaup River joining with Delaware—will be shortly after you launch.

Secluded creeks and marshes hint at an ancient wilderness, and kayaking flat water evokes an intimacy with nature. But the Delaware experience

▶ **Delaware River from Mongaup to Port Jervis**

is decidedly different. The thrills promised by rapids attract throngs of paddlers anxious for excitement and a challenge. Hundreds of people frolicking and floating down the cool water is more suggestive of a carnival ride than an encounter with the wilds of nature.

During most of the six-mile trip, you will paddle through moving flat water. The current is pronounced, flowing inexorably southward toward the Delaware Bay. But you will go as well through sections of flat water and, of course, through some rapids. While in the flat water, keep a lookout for herons and eagles. The birds here are more accustomed to people than in many other places, so you may have an opportunity to get rather close to them. Most likely having been fed in the past by well-meaning boaters, a flock of ducks up ahead flew toward us and skittered across the water inches from our boats. While in the flat water, notice the cliffs that border the river, the pebble beaches, and the islands.

You hear the rapids before you see them. Contending now with choppy water, waves and rocks, you concentrate on paddling, on keeping your

Rafts and kayaks on the Delaware as seen from Hawks Nest Scenic Overlook on SR-97.

boat facing forward—with the current and perpendicular to the waves. Your adrenaline surges. A vee in the water points toward you, signaling a rock close to or at the surface. You go around it, paddling hard, wanting, needing, to control the kayak, to keep the current from turning the boat around. Ahead you see a wave—and then another one. You pull a lot of water with your paddle, meet the first wave, climb it, ride it, dip into the trough and the next wave pours over your bow, soaking you. Another hard pull with the paddle and you are out of the rapids, floating softly on quiet water once again, drenched and laughing.

The railroad bridge signals the halfway point. You paddle some more and, as you approach the cities of Port Jervis and Matamoras, you leave the dramatic cliffs behind. On your right you pass several Matamoras-based river outfitters. Here, most of your fellow paddlers pull off to the right, returning to their cars. Continue on another mile and a half. Ahead of you is the bridge over which US-6 and US-209 cross from New York into Pennsylvania. Look for your car and West End Beach.

A couple of side notes:

You do not need to own your own boat or raft to enjoy the river. Many private outfitters rent rafts, kayaks, and canoes and arrange trips, busing paddlers upstream so they can paddle back.

The Delaware River is a fairly safe place to try out white water. Most of the rapids are class I. There is plenty of information available about every section of the river at the boat accesses and on the Internet. The large number of paddlers means you can easily get assistance should you need it.

Helpful Web sites:

• http://www.nps.gov/archive/upde/boating.htm
gives extensive information about the Upper Delaware River, including a list of boat liveries, weather conditions, river conditions, information on safety, and suggestions on planning a trip.

• http://www.erh.noaa.gov/er/marfc/delaware-upper.htm
gives water levels for the Delaware River and several of its tributaries.

▶ **Delaware River from Mongaup to Port Jervis**

Moodna Creek and Marsh in New Windsor
—Nature against a Backdrop of Industry

O-2

■ **Route:** Entering the Hudson River at Plum Point, head south, then west into Moodna Creek. Paddle around the marsh area, then through the mouth of the creek as far as you can—a little past US-9W.

■ **Total Mileage:** 3+ miles round trip.

■ **Difficulty:** Moderate. **CH C** (See page 18.)

■ **Setting:** Hudson River; marsh; creek wooded but with several active industrial buildings on or near southwest bank.

■ **Hazards:** Currents, tides, weather conditions, and boat traffic on the Hudson always pose some danger to small craft.

■ **Remarks:** Ultimately the creek becomes too shallow to navigate.

On the west bank of the Hudson, Plum Point juts out into the river facing Pollepel Island to the southeast with its locally famous Bannerman Castle. The castle was built by munitions dealer Frank Bannerman, an immigrant from Scotland, to warehouse his stock of surplus weapons. Plum Point is historic in its own right, the site of the first European settlement in Orange County. Now it is home to Kowawese Unique Area, a county park with fishing and small boating access to the Hudson. As with all of the Hudson River paddles, consult a tide chart before going out. A low tide dramatically limits how far you can paddle and what you can see. In addition the Hudson itself is tidal south of Albany and the currents change as a result of both weather—the wind—and the tides.

Directions:
From the New York State Thruway (I-87), take exit 17 to Newburgh following the signs for State Route 17K (SR-17K) East towards Newburgh for 2.3 miles. (Once in Newburgh, the road will be called Broadway.) Turn right onto US-9W (S. Robinson Ave.) Look for a small sign on your left at 2.7 miles for Kowawese Unique Area, right in the middle of a business area with a Toyota dealership, a funeral parlor, and a banquet center. As soon as you make the left turn, you leave the commercial strip and find yourself in a very pretty waterfront park. The park entrance road then splits. To the left is a park for residents of New Windsor only. Bear right to get to the public county park.

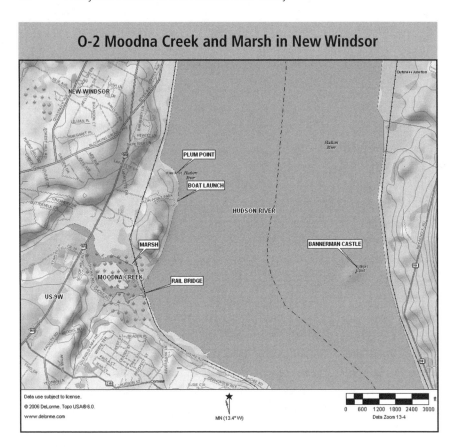

The Paddle:

Put your boat in to the Hudson River to the left of the parking lot (though down a rocky slope, there is a small protected inlet that makes your launch rather easy) and turn towards the south. You need to go out into the river a bit to round a small point jutting into the Hudson from which shore anglers love to fish. The sight of small boats tends to get them rather nervous and excited, so expect to be greeted by not-too-friendly voices warning you in both English and Spanish to watch out for their lines. Alternatively you can avoid the anglers altogether by putting in at the sandy beach to the right of the parking lot. The river is wide here but narrows noticeably as it jogs slightly to the southeast. Most of the larger boats travel between the middle and the eastern side of the river, shielding you somewhat from their wakes.

▶ Moodna Creek and Marsh in New Windsor

Ahead and to your right you will see a railroad bridge. Go under it and you will find yourself in an inlet where the water is calm. The cove is only partially secluded with the north (New Windsor) side a park and the south (Cornwall-on-Hudson) side the commercially zoned Shore Road. Here industry and nature coexist. In this marsh you are likely to see ducks, geese, and herons, their calls sometimes drowned out by the sounds of engines and machines. In fact, an HRNERR (Hudson River National Estuarine Research Reserve) educator who leads canoe trips of young campers suggested that this is one of the best sites on the Hudson for observing wildlife. Accustomed to the sounds of people and motors, the birds here seem less skittish and less likely to fly at the approach of a kayak. Ahead is an island. You can explore the marsh and then continue around the island following the Moodna. The creek continues to follow Shore Road with its excavation company, the Town of Cornwall Sewage Treatment Plant and a technology plant all interspersed among the woods on the southwestern bank. Keep paddling and you will see the

Looking out from the inlet at Plum Point at the railroad bridge
to the Hudson and the Fishkill mountains beyond.

overpass ahead as the creek meanders under the US-9W bridge. Around another bend you leave the road and commercial noise and at last find a truly natural setting. Unfortunately the shallowness of the creek and a slight drop in elevation as it approaches the Hudson prevent you from going much further. Depending on the tide, you can easily portage around this first obstacle, but in a short distance the Moodna will narrow considerably and become rocky and impassable.

If you are wary of paddling on the Hudson River, it is still possible to explore the marsh and creek. Instead of parking at Plum Point, continue on US-9W another quarter of a mile. Look for a sign for the Town of New Windsor kayak ramp. It is on your right behind the New Windsor Water Supply just before the creek.

▶ **Moodna Creek and Marsh in New Windsor**

Neversink River from Cuddebackville to Matamoras, PA
—Beyond the Delaware: White Water with Seclusion

O-3

- **Route:** From launch at Hoag Road, paddle downstream south-south-west to the mouth of the river, where it meets the Delaware. Paddle across the Delaware River to the take-out at Airport Park in Matamoras.
- **Total Mileage**: 11 miles one way.
- **Difficulty:** Most challenging. **O M W** (See page 18.)
- **Setting:** Mostly forested. Steep and rugged banks on much of the eastern bank have prevented development and kept the area natural and pristine.
- **Hazards:** Class I rapids, seasonally some class II rapids. (On international class I-VI scale, class I are the easiest. Class I—moving water with few riffles and small waves. Few or no obstructions. Class II—Easy rapids with waves up to three feet and wide clear channels that are obvious. This, according to the American Canoe Association.)
- **Remarks:** Requires two vehicles. The gradient drop over the 11 miles is about 95 feet, an average of 8.6 feet per mile. Two thirds of the elevation change is in the first half of the course—12.5 feet of drop per mile. The first half of the paddle is, therefore, the most daunting. It is also the shallowest. When water levels are not sufficiently high, you may need to pull your boat around the shallowest parts. You can cut off some of the shallowest and the most challenging section by putting in near the Guymard Turnpike overpass. From the County Route 80 (CR-80) bridge on, the river is much quieter, varying from virtually flat water to moving flat water with riffles and occasional small rapids. Review "The Limitations of a Paddling Guide."

Perhaps you paddled the Delaware River and were thrilled by its rapids and waves, by the splashing and general frivolity. You'd like to try a river with a similar roller-coaster ride—but without the hordes of tourists and the amusement-park feel. The stretch of the Neversink River between Cuddebackville and Port Jervis, though much narrower than the Delaware, combines both the challenge and scenic beauty of the Delaware River with the seclusion of wilderness.

O-3 Neversink River from Cuddebackville to Matamoras, PA

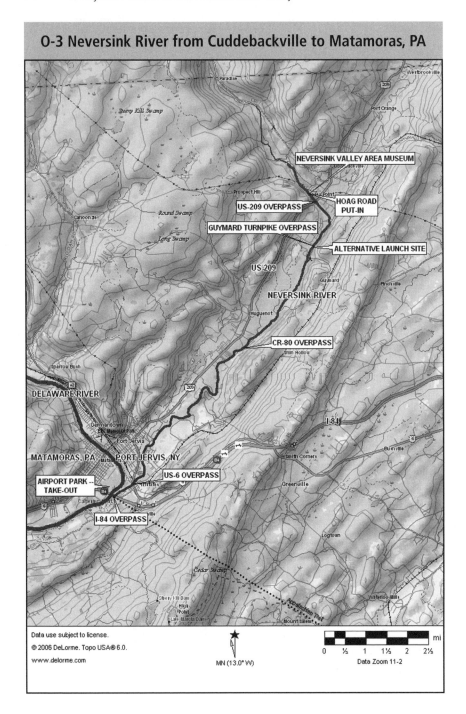

▶ **Neversink River from Cuddebackville to Matamoras, PA**

The Neversink River has a rich history. On its banks and in its waters, a New York fisherman, Theodore Gordon, developed the uniquely American fly, one adapted to its lively waters, and helped popularize the sport of fly fishing.

The Neversink Dam in Sullivan County, built in the mid-twentieth century, diverts most of the river's waters—a startling 80 percent, in fact—and sends the collected waters through a gravity-feed tunnel to the Rondout Reservoir, where it mixes with other water from the Delaware watershed before beginning its long trek south as part of the New York City Water Supply. According to the Nature Conservancy, an environmental group dedicated to preserving bio-diversity, the water of the Neversink is the purest source of drinking water for the city.

The Neversink has a unique place in the history of the environmental movement as well. A dam, constructed first to redirect river water to the canal connecting the Delaware and Hudson rivers, and added to later to help provide hydroelectric power—then not used for over fifty years—has recently been torn down. With the dam down, fish and other species now travel upstream to spawn. This joint effort of the Nature Conservancy and the Army Corps of Engineers is the first dam in New York State torn down solely for the health of the local ecology.

Directions to the Airport Park take-out in Matamoras:
Take I-84 East past Port Jervis and over the Delaware River into Pennsylvania. Exit immediately (exit #53), turning right onto Pennsylvania Avenue (US-209 North, US-6 East). Continue for .25 mile. Turn right on Tenth Street. The street ends in less than half a mile at Airport Park. Turn left onto the park road, a former runway, and then make your first right down a dirt road leading to several fishing accesses along the bank of the Delaware. Leave one vehicle here.

Directions to the Cuddebackville launch area
from Airport Park:
Go back out on Tenth Street and turn right onto US-209 (Pennsylvania Avenue). Follow US-209 as it crosses the Delaware, jogs right then left through Port Jervis, and begins it northeast course towards Kingston. At just under 9 miles, you will see an "Entering Cuddebackville" sign and cross over the Neversink River. Take your first left onto Hoag Road. There

are several places along this road from which you can park and launch. We launched directly across from the Neversink Valley Area Museum.

The Paddle:

The river runs by the side of Hoag Road. From Hoag Road the launch is fairly easy, but the water is moving from the start and tends to be shallow. If water levels are not high, your kayak will likely scrape rocks along bottom. But if you do this trip after a heavy rain or after the spring thaw, you should have no problem. After the first bridge the river is a bit deeper, though from time to time throughout the first half—between Cuddebackville and the CR-80 bridge—you will again encounter rocks and shallow water.

Once you cross under US-209, the river passes by Myers Grove, a small community on the west bank of the Neversink that was formerly a vacation community of modest homes and double-wides. Over the years most of them were winterized and became year-round housing. That is, until April 2005, when the Neversink flooded. To this day most of these houses are no longer occupied and, in fact, many of them are condemned. You cannot see the devastation from a kayak; the raised bank blocks the houses from view. After you go under a second bridge, the Guymard Turnpike overpass, the river leaves roads behind for the next three miles. The wooded banks seem wild and secluded. You might notice Nature Conservancy Preserve signs along the shore. The Conservancy has acquired 550 acres adjacent to the river in an effort to protect almost thirty rare species that live here and to safeguard their habitat.

After the CR-80 overpass the river becomes much tamer; the flow slows and you paddle harder. You pass occasional houses, fairly well hidden for the most part by the woods. The river bends and turns more now as you approach Port Jervis. You skirt the city for the final mile and a half, eventually passing first under US-6, then under I-84. You have just left the mouth of the Neversink. To get to your car, cross the Delaware, paddling hard against the current into Matamoras.

▶ **Neversink River from Cuddebackville to Matamoras, PA**

Otter Kill in Washingtonville
—Pulsing with Life

O-4

■ **Route:** Put in on Twin Arch Road less than a half mile north of State Route 208 (SR-208). Go upstream a mile. Turn around as the creek gets shallower and rockier. Head back, passing the put-in point. Go less than half a mile to the top of a dam. Return to your car.

■ **Total Mileage:** 3 miles round trip.

■ **Difficulty:** Easy.

■ **Setting:** Marsh, woods, occasional houses.

■ **Hazards:** Heading downstream, you shortly approach the top of a dam. Listen for it; it is not marked.

■ **Remarks:** Short trip includes a variety of scenery. Marsh area near put-in is good for wildlife viewing. Riffles require short and easy portage.

Look at a map of Orange County. Dozens of small streams, creeks, brooks and "kills" traverse the county. You consider putting your kayak into one of them. You look for one that offers access that is relatively easy, water that is fairly calm and sufficiently deep, and a setting that is picturesque. Try the Otter Kill, just outside Washingtonville in the town of Hamptonburgh.

Directions:

This section of the Otter Kill is just off SR-208. Take I-84 to exit 5. Go south on SR-208 for about 6.5 miles. Turn left onto Twin Arch Road. (Or, from I-87 get off at exit 16. Take US-6 West [SR-17] for 4 miles, then SR-208 North through the village of Washingtonville for a total of a little over 8 miles. Turn right on Twin Arch Road.)

Along this stretch the Otter Kill runs next to Twin Arch Road. While there are no official launch sites here for the creek, there are at least three places to pull off, places often used by local fishermen, which allow for easy access to the water. I pulled into the first of the three, just under half a mile from the intersection with SR-208 and right before an imposing, abandoned railroad bridge.

O-4 Otter Kill in Washingtonville

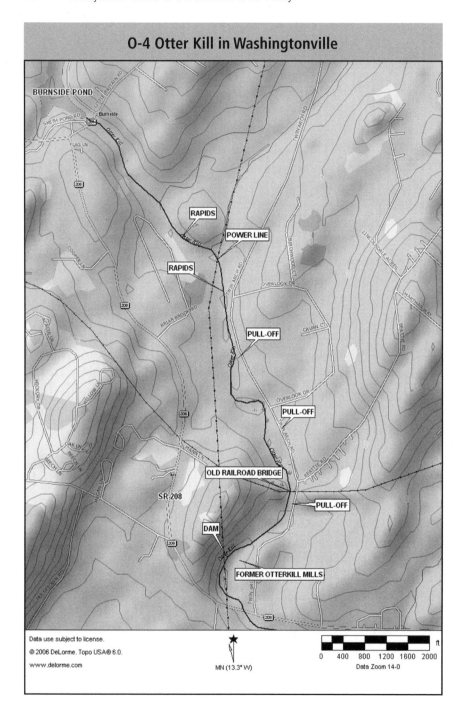

BURNSIDE POND

Burnside

SMITH POND RD

FLAG LN

COOPER LN

RAPIDS

POWER LINE

RAPIDS

PULL-OFF

PULL-OFF

OLD RAILROAD BRIDGE

SR 208

PULL-OFF

DAM

FORMER OTTERKILL MILLS

Data use subject to license.

© 2006 DeLorme. Topo USA® 6.0.

www.delorme.com

MN (13.3° W)

0   400   800   1200   1600   2000   ft

Data Zoom 14-0

▶ **Otter Kill in Washingtonville**

The Paddle:

A small clearing near the creek edge makes for a simple launch. Turning upstream, to the right, I paddled under an arched concrete railroad bridge. The darkness within contrasted with the sunlight without. I was struck by the harmony of seemingly disparate forces. The road, the hallmark of civilization and man's intrusion into nature, runs right beside the stream, pulsing with life, the essence of nature. The purple flowers of the native pickerel weed stood erect against a background of the invasive purple loosestrife; both plants help realize the wetland environment, home to so many species. A large deer came down to the edge of the creek to drink and cool down as eastern painted turtles climbed up onto every protruding rock and log to warm themselves in the afternoon sun. Fearful of predators, they slipped off into the water as I paddled past while a red-tailed hawk landed on a branch overhanging the water, wary, searching for prey. I observed the dramatic changes in both the scenery and in the creek itself. At first my kayak floated over submerged plants browning in late summer, swaying as I passed through the marsh. Trying to assess the depth of the water, I plunged my paddle into the creek bottom, which was soft and gave to the touch. Half a mile into the trip, the muddy bottom gave way to rocks, and the marsh to woods.

Here the Otter Kill was not even the four feet deep I had measured earlier, and the shallowness combined with the rocky bottom created riffles. My kayak scraped bottom. I decided not to turn back yet. Instead I put my feet into the chilly water, pushed my kayak over the rocks, and hopped back in. I paddled over the smooth surface of the calm water, and in another quarter of a mile or so the woods opened up where trees had been cut for a power line that crosses the creek. I heard the sound of water up ahead, and in the distance I made out a churning of the water. I had come to another riffle. It would be another easy portage, but the creek was running shallower here, and I decided to head back. I thought that perhaps another day I would return and make it all the way to the dam below Burnside Pond.

On my return paddle, I passed the pull-off where I'd parked the truck and paddled downstream further. I heard the water roaring over the dam before I saw it—it is hard to see a dam from its top when you are low in a kayak. You see rather the illusion of a shelf of water, a straight horizon line interrupting the flow of the stream. I felt no pull towards the dam—

there was no danger here of being dragged by the current. I got to the far side and faced the house that sits opposite on the water's edge. This was once a mill; the original structure dates back to 1721. Though it was remodeled in the 1960s as a home, this was, in fact, when it shut down in 1931, the last grist mill in operation in Orange County.

With nowhere else to paddle, I headed back.

Paddling under the railroad bridge on the Otter Kill.

▶ Otter Kill in Washingtonville

Wallkill River in Warwick
—Through the Black Dirt Region and the Cheechunk Canal
O-5

- **Route:** From the Oil City Road boat access, go northeast, downstream, as the Wallkill first winds and then continues straight in its altered course through an agricultural area of Orange County. Take-out is on Celery Avenue.
- **Total Mileage:** Just under 10 miles one way.
- **Difficulty:** Moderate to challenging. **R D P O M** (See page 18.)
- **Setting:** Woods and farmland.
- **Hazards:** This is mostly flat water and moving flat water with two or three small rapids.
- **Remarks:** Requires two vehicles. Though the canal portion is sufficiently deep to paddle at any time, the rest is easier to paddle when water levels are not extremely low. This first section of the Wallkill River is easily navigable only in one direction. The current going upstream is manageable, but tiring; two sets of rapids would require portaging to return to the Oil City Road launch. In addition, deadfall may require a brief portage.

The southwest corner of Orange County has an intriguing history. Thousands of years ago a vast, shallow lake, the result of melting glaciers, spread out over much of the area. When the climate warmed after the last ice age, the lake eventually dried out. Where it receded, dense vegetation grew. However, the Wallkill River, which wound its way circuitously through the region in a number of narrow and shallow channels, frequently flooded. Hundreds of years of cycles of lush growth followed by periods of flooding resulted in an accumulation of rich layers of decaying matter. This became the rich, dark soil that has given the "Black Dirt Region" its name.

Early settlers tried to farm the land, but with little success because of the constant flooding. Finally, in the early 1800s, area farmers succeeded in building the Cheechunk Canal, deepening and straightening the course of the Wallkill. However, not everyone supported the canal's construction. In fact, rerouting the river caused great hardship to those who were dependent on mills that had been built adjacent to its banks and used its flow for power. This kicked off the "muskrat and beaver wars"—battles between two conflicting ways of life—with

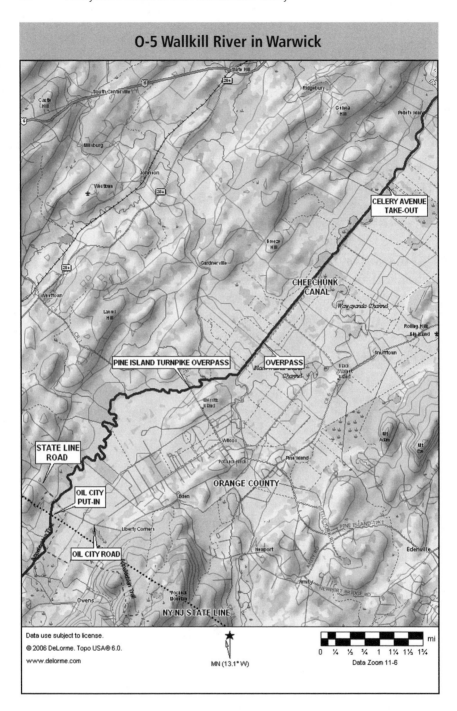

O-5 Wallkill River in Warwick

CELERY AVENUE TAKE-OUT

CHEECHUNK CANAL

PINE ISLAND TURNPIKE OVERPASS

OVERPASS

STATE LINE ROAD

ORANGE COUNTY

OIL CITY PUT-IN

OIL CITY ROAD

NY-NJ STATE LINE

Data use subject to license.
© 2006 DeLorme. Topo USA® 6.0.
www.delorme.com

MN (13.1° W)

0   ¼   ½   ¾   1   1¼   1½   1¾   mi

Data Zoom 11-6

▶ **Wallkill River in Warwick**

the surreptitious construction of dams along the canal to redirect the water to the original channels. Late in the nineteenth century these "wars" were eventually decided by court rulings that favored the farmers. During the Great Depression the Civilian Conservation Corps, with the dual goal of putting large numbers of young, unemployed men to work and improving the natural resources of the country, again dug out and reinforced the canal.

The name of the road from which you launch, Oil City Road, also reflects some of the county's unique history. John D. Rockefeller's Esso (Standard Oil, now Exxon) corporation built a pipeline from Olean, New York, to Bayonne, New Jersey, crossing the Wallkill River here. That pipeline, the first in the United States, and a nearby oil pumping station lent the road its name.

Now, from the Oil City Road boat access, maintained by the Wallkill River National Wildlife Refuge, you can experience both the original winding, narrow channels favored by "the muskrats" and the man-made, straight-as-an-arrow canal favored by "the beaver."

Directions to Celery Avenue:
Before launching your kayak from Oil City Road, you will want to drop off a second vehicle on Celery Avenue—one of several nearby roads named after regional crops. From I-84, get off at exit 3. Take US-6 (State Route 17M) East for 1.3 miles. Turn right onto County Route 12 (CR-12), also called Lower Road. Stay on CR-12 for 1.9 miles, turning left onto CR-37 (Pellets Island Road). You will cross the Wallkill River, then pass Old Celery Avenue. Take the next right onto Celery Avenue, a dead-end road paralleling the Wallkill River. At 1.5 miles a gravel road goes off to the right. You will see Department of Environmental Conservation and Department of Public Works signs warning against dumping or driving on flood-control lands. These signs are visible from the river—use them as a marker when paddling later. There is room to pull off on the edge of Celery Avenue and you will be able to walk your kayak out easily. But realize that this in not an official boat access maintained for the public.

Directions from Celery Avenue to Oil City Road boat access:
Go back to CR-37 (Maple Ave.) Turn left, staying on CR-37 for just over half a mile. Turn left onto CR-12 and continue for 6 miles until it

ends. Bear right onto CR-1. At just under a mile, turn left onto Lower Road. Stay on Lower Road until it intersects with State Line Road (2.4 miles). State Line Road becomes Oil City Road as it crosses the Wallkill River. As soon as you cross the river, pull into the parking lot on your left.

The Paddle:
Trees shade the launch area, a favorite spot for local anglers. Turn right and allow the current to help you downstream away from the National Refuge. The transition from public land to private land is subtle. Though not protected, the tree-lined edges of the river seem unspoiled; the river is murky, but free of refuse. Here the Wallkill meanders as it traverses rich farmland. No suburban sprawl, no houses mar the scenery—no factories, no mills, no dams. As you continue to paddle generally northward, you will gradually notice more fields of corn beyond the bank and perhaps an irrigation pump, signs of the agriculture-based economy of the region. Occasional sounds of farm machinery and the four bridges you paddle under are other hints of civilization—the Pine Island Turnpike overpass is the only one with an occasional car.

The river twists repeatedly, and around some of those initial turns within the first mile of your trip you encounter the first of two places with rapids. Your kayak dips down slightly and speeds up as the flow pushes you ahead. Some yards further, another easy rapids, and then a mile further another slight descent—none of them dangerous, but all impossible to muscle back—making this a one-way paddle. This section of the Wallkill is fairly narrow and partially shaded by the trees growing on its banks. The river sides of their root structure have been eroded by the current; some of them tilt precipitously, forming a picturesque canopy. And, on occasion, a tree falls, blocking the river. As we paddled this ten-mile section of the river, Joe and I encountered only one place that required portaging. I dragged my boat over the tree trunk; he pulled and carried his through brush on the bank. After a few minutes and some serious exertion, we were again on our way.

This remote section of the Wallkill River, far from cities, set back from villages, offers a great opportunity for wildlife watching. We flushed geese, herons, and ducks and watched several red-tailed hawks as they rose and veered and soared above.

▶ **Wallkill River in Warwick**

The Pine Island Turnpike overpass marks the halfway point of the trip. In this stretch the river turns a bit less as it heads eastward. Watch for a marsh and a creek off on your left. That is Rutgers Creek, known in these parts for its trout. Go a little over a half mile farther and the Wallkill turns noticeably to the left into the Cheechunk Canal. Here the river is deep, slightly wider and improbably, almost shockingly, straight as it cuts through miles of farmed land, sometimes visible from the river, often hidden by trees edging the banks.

Paddle the Cheechunk section of the Wallkill, and in five miles you will see, on your right, electric wires signaling a road and the Department of Public Works "No Dumping" sign. Should you miss the landmark, you will pass houses and a farm complex with large tractor trailers parked across the street. And if you go another half a mile, you will approach a rather challenging rapids. Return to the DPW sign and the take-out.

The Wallkill deepens and straightens as it flows through the man-made Cheechunk Canal.

| 0-6– |
| 0-8 |

Orange County
Ponds and Lakes

0-6 Harriman State Park Lakes

Harriman State Park with its 44,000 acres and 31 lakes and reservoirs is the largest park managed by the Palisades Interstate Park Commission. If you buy an annual PIPC boat permit, you may take your kayak or canoe into any of six of the beautiful Harriman lakes in Orange County. Some of the lakes charge a daily use fee; they all accept the Empire Pass in lieu of that charge. Some of the parks lock the boat access and require in addition the purchase of a key.

Directions to the park:

■ **From the South:** Take I-87 to exit 15A. Get onto State Route 17 North. Take your first right (2.8 miles) onto Seven Lakes Drive, heading northeast.

■ **From the North:** Take I-87 to exit 16. Turn left at light and follow the signs for US-6 East. Stay on US-6 for 6.4 miles. Turn right onto Seven Lakes Drive, heading southwest.

Web site:

• http://nysparks.state.ny.us/parks/info.asp?parkID=143
gives basic information about the park facilities, directions, and contact information.

Island Pond in Tuxedo

■ **How to get there:** From New York State Thruway (either exit 15A or exit 16), take State Route 17. Turn east onto Arden Valley Road. The locked park entrance is 1.4 miles ahead on your right.

■ **Where to put in:** Right beyond the parking lot is a paved ramp leading to the pond. The actual water access is not quite so easy, however. You must contend with uneven rocks and unsure footing.

■ **Remarks:** To limit the usage and preserve the intimacy of the 53-acre Island Pond, keys are sold only during a two-week period in March.

▶ **Orange County Ponds and Lakes**

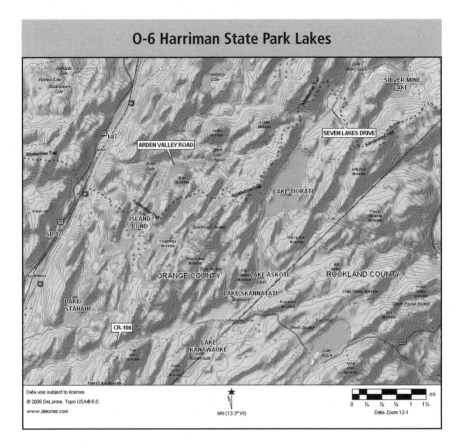

O-6 Harriman State Park Lakes

Web site:

• http://www.dec.state.ny.us/website/dfwmr/fish/lakemaps/islapdmap.
pdf offers a map of Island Pond. Though not meant for navigational
use, the map gives water surface area, depths, contours, and species of fish found.

Lake Askoti in Tuxedo

■ **How to get there:** Take Seven Lakes Drive. Lake Askoti is just north
of the county boundary on the east side of the road about halfway
between US-6 and State Route 17.

■ **Where to put in:** A pull-off for one car only lies adjacent to the southern tip of the lake. Here you can unload your boat. Shared parking for this lake and Lake Skannatati is across the road.

■ **Remarks:** Compared to some of the other Harriman lakes, this one is relatively small—43 acres. The entire lake is visible from the road.

Web site:

• http://www.dec.state.ny.us/website/dfwmr/fish/lakemaps/lkaskmap.pdf offers a map of Lake Askoti. Though not meant for navigational use, the map gives water surface area, depths, contours, and species of fish found.

Lake Kanawauke in Tuxedo

■ **How to get there:** Take Seven Lakes Drive to its intersection with County Route 106 (CR-106) just south of lakes Askoti and Skannatati. Turn onto CR-106. Right after you turn, on your left you will see a drive down to the launch area. The main parking lot is a hundred feet beyond.

■ **Where to put in:** Use the drive for loading and unloading your boats. It allows for easy access to the lake. Then park in the official lot.

■ **Remarks:** The 79-acre lake with its jagged shoreline offers a varied and picturesque setting. Near the launch, the area is mowed and manicured. But many fingers of this lake extend on both sides of CR-106, some quite rustic with water lilies and miniature islands.

Lake Skannatati in Tuxedo

■ **How to get there:** Take Seven Lakes Drive. Lake Skannatati is just north of the county boundary on the west side of the road about halfway between US-6 and State Route 17.

■ **Where to put in:** Descend to the lake via a short park road. A gently sloped, beach-like access makes putting in easy.

■ **Remarks:** Though at 37 acres this is the smallest of the Harriman boating lakes in Orange County, the descent from Seven Lakes Drive gives it a bit more of a feel of seclusion than its sister lake across the road.

▶ **Orange County Ponds and Lakes**

Web site:

• http://www.dec.state.ny.us/website/dfwmr/fish/lakemaps/lkskanmap. pdf offers a map of Lake Skannatati. Though not meant for navigational use, the map gives water surface area, depths, contours, and species of fish found.

Lake Stahahe in Tuxedo

■ **How to get there:** From Seven Lakes Drive, take County Route 106 west for a little under 4 miles. Look for the small "Lake Stahahe Foreman Road" sign on your right. This leads to the parking area for the lake, which is chained and locked.

■ **Where to put in:** There is a dock about thirty feet below the parking lot. You need to carry your boat down. Footing is a bit uneven.

■ **Remarks:** Access to this 85-acre lake requires the purchase of a key.

Web site:

• http://www.dec.state.ny.us/website/dfwmr/fish/lakemaps/lkstahmap. pdf offers a map of Lake Stahahe. Though not meant for navigational use, the map gives water surface area, depths, contours, and species of fish found.

Lake Tiorati in Tuxedo

■ **How to get there:** Lake Tiorati lies adjacent to Seven Lakes Drive between Lake Askoti and Silver Mine Lake. Take Seven Lakes Drive to Tiorati Circle, the place where the northernmost tip of the lake touches the road. Turn onto Tiorati Brook Road, which does not quite circle the lake, but tends to follow the shoreline. Boat loading and unloading and lake access is on your right, one mile from the circle, adjacent to the Tiorati Dam. Boat parking is on the other side of the road.

■ **Where to put in:** From the loading zone a concrete ramp leads directly to the water's edge.

■ **Remarks:** A key is needed to access the chained launch site. Lake Tiorati is the most developed lake in the park with a beach, picnic areas, and camping, but the 297-acre lake easily accommodates the many visitors. The lake is sprawling and beautiful, and the launch area is far from the busy beach and picnic grounds.

Web site:

• http://www.dec.state.ny.us/website/dfwmr/fish/lakemaps/lktiormap. pdf offers a map of Lake Tiorati. Though not meant for navigational use, the map gives water surface area, depths, contours, and species of fish found.

Silver Mine Lake in Woodbury

■ **How to get there:** Take Seven Lakes Drive. The lake is 1.5 miles south of the intersection with US-6 on the east side of the drive.
■ **Where to put in:** You can drive in front of the parking lots down towards the lake to unload your boat right by the water. Then park in the main area.
■ **Remarks:** Only a tip of Lake Silvermine touches the road. So, against a backdrop of mountains much of the 82-acre lake, edged with lilies and other underwater plants, offers seclusion.

Web site:

• http://www.dec.state.ny.us/website/dfwmr/fish/lakemaps/sminlkmap. pdf offers a map of Silver Mine Lake. Though not meant for navigational use, the map gives water surface area, depths, contours, and species of fish found.

▶ **Orange County Ponds and Lakes**

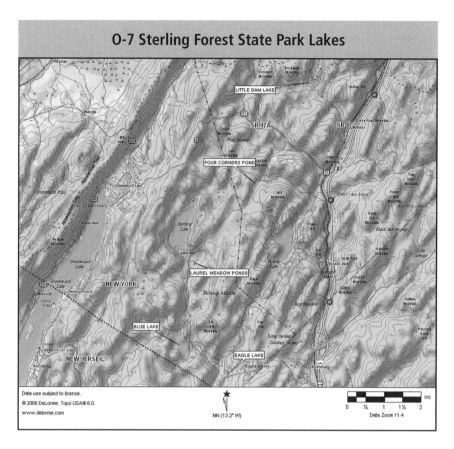

0-7 Sterling Forest State Park Lakes

Sterling Forest is one of the newest state parks. Original planning for the area focused on the idea of creating a great place to work, live, and play. With that in mind, some fledgling developers and some corporations, most notably IBM, began to build. When environmentalists raised the public's awareness as to the importance of protecting our watersheds, New York State bought up land and created Sterling Forest State Park. The park has five lakes that permit boating. They are Blue Lake, Little Dam Lake, Eagle Lake, Laurel Meadows Ponds and Four Corners Pond. The last three are so small—under 10 acres each—that they are hardly worth the effort of transporting and launching a kayak. All require purchase of both an annual Palisades Interstate Park Commission permit and a Sterling Forest State Park permit.

Directions to the park:
From the South: Take I-87 to exit 15A. Get onto State Route 17 (SR-17) North. Take your first left (1.5 miles) onto Silver Mine Road, also called County Route 72 (CR-72), heading west for 3 miles to the intersection with CR-84, which traverses the park.

From the North: Take I-87 to exit 16. Follow the signs for SR-17 South. Stay on SR-17 for 8 miles. Turn right onto SR-17A. After just under a mile and a half, turn left onto CR-84, which traverses the park.

Blue Lake in Warwick

- **How to get there:** Take County Route 84 to the southern portion of the park. The road runs adjacent to a corner of the lake.
- **Where to put in:** Access is easy via a gently sloped launch area.
- **Remarks:** The 108-acre lake is rather pretty, but the adjacent corporate building dwarfs the trees and overwhelms the natural landscape.

Little Dam Lake in Tuxedo

- **How to get there:** From State Route 17 turn onto Orange Turnpike (County Route 19) North. Turn left onto Bramertown Road. The lake is on your right.
- **Where to put in:** You must carry your boat from the parking lot and down over a rocky embankment.
- **Remarks:** The unique shape of this small, 37-acre lake with its many corners and crannies and its beautiful marsh setting might make it worth the difficult launch, a steep and slippery descent over loose rocks to the water's edge. The road to the Little Dam Lake is locked, and access requires the additional purchase of a key.

▶ **Orange County Ponds and Lakes**

Web site:

• http://www.greenwoodlake.org/SFGeneral.htm
  offers information about the history and recreation facilities
  of the park.

0-8 Winding Hills County Park in Montgomery

▨ **How to get there:** Exit I-84 at State Route 208 (SR-208) North (exit #5).
  After just over a mile turn left off of SR-208 onto SR-17K. Continue on
  SR-17K through the village of Montgomery for 2 miles. Turn right onto
  Old SR-17K and into the park.
▨ **Where to put in:** Take the road into the park. Turn left, following the
  signs to the boathouse.
▨ **Remarks:** This pretty park, owned and maintained by Orange County,
  offers camping, boating, fishing, and hiking. They rent rowboats and
  paddleboats, but you are permitted to launch your own boat. Woods
  and park grounds surround the lake, creating a rustic feel.

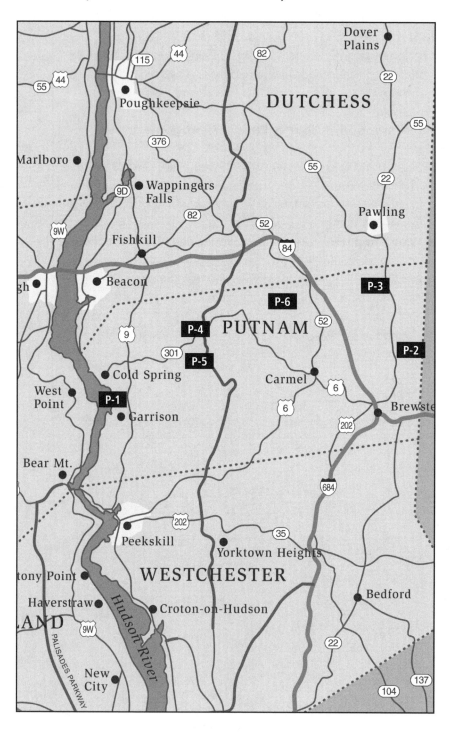

3

Putnam County

The rivers are our brothers. They quench our thirst. They carry our canoes and feed our children. You must give to the rivers the kindness you would give to any brother.

Chief Seattle

P-1 Constitution Marsh in Cold Spring
—Birds and Wild Rice

- **Route:** After putting in to the Hudson River at Cold Spring, turn south and enter the preserve under the railroad bridge. Here, paddle through waterways running throughout the marsh.
- **Total Mileage:** Varies according to your discretion and time—up to 5+ miles round trip.
- **Difficulty:** Moderate. **CH C** (See page 18.)
- **Setting:** Hudson River, marsh and shrub forests.
- **Hazards:** Currents, tides, weather conditions, and boat traffic on the Hudson always pose some danger to small craft. Tidal considerations: during low tide, the water recedes dramatically and some of the channels become impassable; at high tide the water level approaches the bottom of the bridge and access to the marsh may be limited.
- **Remarks:** Clearly marked signs advise that the sanctuary is closed seasonally for the protection of bird populations.

The five tidal marshes that border the Hudson River offer a unique opportunity for close-up and personal wildlife watching. The wetlands provide a refuge for many species of birds. Some migrate north and nest here during the warm months; others, like the American black duck, winter in the marsh. The National Audubon Society manages this environmental site for New York State, whose Office of Parks, Recreation, and Historic Preservation owns the land. Channels of water crisscross the marsh; most of these channels, incidentally, are man-made, an early nineteenth-century attempt by Henry Warner to construct rice paddies and harvest wild rice. Perhaps the rice, though native to the region, could not keep out the more dominant cattails, arrow arum, and pickerelweed. Or maybe the brackish water that during the warmer and drier seasons reaches as far north as Cold Spring prevented the rice from flourishing. In any case, Warner's attempts failed. The channels he constructed have lasted, however, and offer a great way to see the marsh. High tide provides much more access to the area and, in fact, the Audubon Society urges visitors not to enter at all near low tide when the channels empty out and many become impassable.

▶ Constitution Marsh in Cold Spring

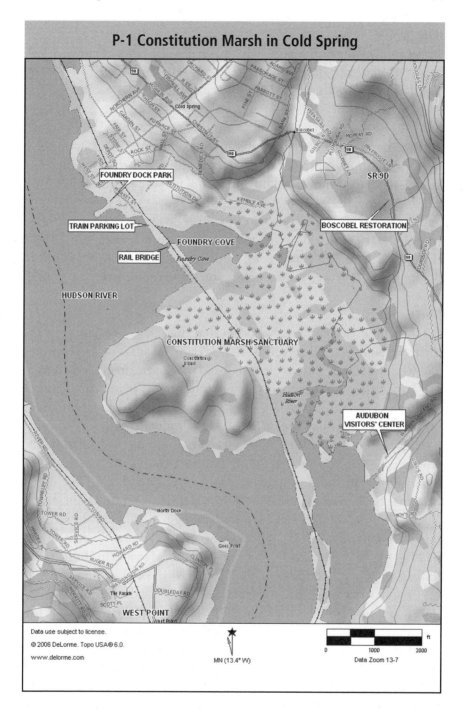

P-1 Constitution Marsh in Cold Spring

Directions:

To get to Constitution Marsh, which lies directly below Boscobel Restoration where the Hudson Valley Shakespeare Festival performs every summer, from I-84 take exit 11 onto State Route 9D (SR-9D) South. Stay on SR-9D for 8 miles into the town of Cold Spring. Turn right onto SR-301 (Main Street). (Or, from the east side of the Hudson, get off the Taconic State Parkway in Putnam County at SR-301 and take it west for 8.5 miles into the village of Cold Spring, where it will become Main Street.) Continue on Main Street until you can go no further. Turn left onto Lunn Terrace, which in one block turns to the right, and then make a left onto Market Street. On your right is the newly renovated Foundry Dock Park with river access, a boat-launch area, and limited parking. If the parking area is full, unload and then continue on into the railroad lot, where on weekends you can park for free.

The Paddle:

The first time I came here, believing that the marsh was south of the town, we paddled in that direction. There are no signposts in the water, and with the solitude of a spring weekday, there were no other boaters to ask. Fortunately the river was calm and the currents were manageable as Kendra and I made our way around Constitution Island and through the mighty Hudson in our twelve-foot kayaks. We paddled over two miles basking in the sun and the sheer pleasure of the place, cradled by the Hudson Highlands with West Point on the opposite shore. When we had finally passed the military academy, we turned around, fairly certain we had somehow missed the sanctuary. Just as the Cold Spring train station again came clearly into view, totally baffling me—how could we have missed it, after all—Kendra, pointing to a railroad bridge adjacent to the parking lot, said, "It couldn't be under that bridge, could it?" It could have been under that bridge, and, of course, it was.

So, put in to the Hudson River and turn left, heading south, and hug the shoreline. Go under the railroad bridge. If it is high tide, as it was for us that day, you may need to get extremely low in your boat and use the struts on the bottom of the bridge to both steer and move yourself forward into Foundry Cove. You can see the marsh ahead of you to the right. Close to 300 acres of pristine wetland, thousands of years old, lie before you. As you wend your way through the maze of water channels,

▶ **Constitution Marsh in Cold Spring**

In the foreground pickerel weed blooms in Constitution Marsh, behind that
the tree line, and in the background haze, the Mid-Hudson Highlands.

take care not to disturb the vegetation, which hides and houses a variety
of wildlife. Paddle in and enjoy.

The Audubon Society offers guided canoe trips through the marsh
starting at the visitors' center on Indian Brook Road. They provide
canoes, life jackets, and a wealth of knowledge about the human history, the natural history, and the wildlife of the area. On a return trip
to the marsh, Eric Lind, the director of the Audubon Center, guided
me through the channels pointing out a kingfisher, an eagle, a muskrat
lodge, and a marsh wren nest. From him I learned that in its twenty-six
years of operation between 1953 and 1979 the Marathon Battery Factory
had dumped toxic cadmium and nickel into Foundry Cove polluting
the sediment and the water. Under environmental pressure supported
by the Clean Water Act of 1970, Marathon eventually relocated. Years
later the cadmium pollution resulted in Foundry Cove's designation as

a Superfund site—an area so toxic that the federal government would oversee its cleanup. In the early 1990s the eastern portion of Foundry Cove was dredged and replanted. As with much of the Hudson, the terrible pollution here has been reversed. Yet it may take many years to completely reestablish the native ecology.

When you eventually decide to call it a day, consider a walking tour of the local area. Cold Spring is a picturesque town, with its train depot and small shops a reminder of a bygone era. On Saturdays you can take a shuttle bus from the south end of the train station parking lot to Constitution Island, an island belonging to West Point and rich with the history of the American Revolution, and which is surrounded on three sides by the Hudson and on the back by the marsh.

Helpful Web sites:

- http://www.audubon.org/chapter/ny/ny/cmac.htm
  gives the mission statement of the Audubon conservation effort at Constitution Marsh, information on their education center, school programs, and naturalist-led canoe trips.

- http://ny.audubon.org/iba/constitution.html
  offers information about the sanctuary, the birds found there, and conservation issues.

- http://www.dec.state.ny.us/website/dfwmr/wildlife/bca/cons_mgs.html has some basic information on the marsh and the way it is managed.

- http://hhr.highlands.com/marshyr.html
  gives some history of the marsh and a month-by-month October to March synopsis of the natural environment.

- http://web.cecs.pdx.edu/~fishw/ECR-FoundryCove01.htm
  gives a history of the pollution and cleanup of Foundry Cove.

▶ **Constitution Marsh in Cold Spring**

East Branch Croton River—Starting from Green Chimneys —*The Raw Pull of the Great Swamp*

P-2

- ■ **Route:** Beginning at Green Chimneys launch site, paddle upstream towards Patterson. Alternatively, head south under County Route 65 (CR-65), also called Doansburg Road, towards the East Branch Reservoir.
- ■ **Total Mileage:** Variable—up to several miles round trip.
- ■ **Difficulty:** Easy to moderate. (If you go south and choose to portage around obstacles, the course could prove challenging. **R P** (See page 18.)
- ■ **Setting:** The Great Swamp: floodplain forest.
- ■ **Hazards:** Heading north, beaver dams; heading south, riffles, deadfall, and dams.
- ■ **Remarks:** Paddle upstream and northward through "lake" area of river toward State Route 22 (SR-22) overpass. Or, seasonally, follow the river southward. Should you try the southern paddle, note that there is a decided southward current with sporadic riffles. However, under normal conditions the current is not so strong as to prevent a return trip upstream. An occasional log jam, frequent beaver dams, and downed trees could well require portages. Do not enter the reservoir itself. To protect its water supply New York City does not allow paddling in its reservoirs.

Before setting out to paddle new territory, I pored over maps of the Hudson River Valley and was immediately struck by the amount of blue on the maps of the smallest of the counties. While Putnam County is less than half the size of Greene or Columbia, less than a third the size of Dutchess or Orange, and less than a quarter the size of Ulster County, 6 percent of its total area is water—more than double the percentage of those larger, neighboring counties. Putnam's unique geography, with its proximity to New York City and with its plentiful rivers, streams, lakes, ponds, and now reservoirs, contains the key to its past. The county's location on the Hudson River led to its commercial growth in the eighteenth century. Overlooking the river, its famous Hudson Highlands were of strategic importance during the American Revolution. When industry declined in the region in the nineteenth century, Putnam County's geography once again played a significant role, this time in its recovery. New York City, with its need for a vast

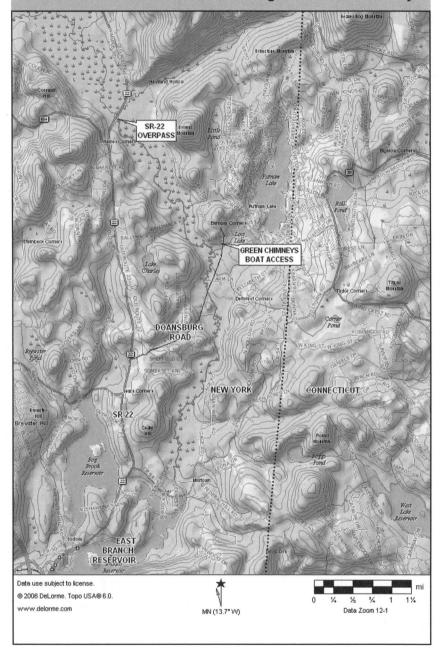

P-2 East Branch Croton River—Starting from Green Chimneys

▶ **East Branch Croton River—Starting from Green Chimneys**

and reliable water supply, looked to Putnam with its abundance of clean water. The city built reservoirs and thus launched Putnam's special role today as a major watershed providing a sizable portion of the city's water and supporting simultaneously a large wetland habitat for a great variety of wildlife.

What intrigued me most in the articles I read was the vast area in the eastern section of the county dubbed "The Great Swamp," a swamp that runs through the two townships of Southeast and Patterson and northward into Dutchess County. Huge and contiguous to the burgeoning suburbia around New York City, the swamp is subject to all the pressures of mushrooming development. Yet to a large degree the communities surrounding the Great Swamp, government agencies, and an array of nonprofit organizations have embraced the protection of this natural wonder.

The awesome power of Hurricane Katrina and the awful devastation to New Orleans in her wake should serve as a warning to us of the importance of wetlands and swamps. The fact that New Orleans lies below sea level protected by a system of levees alone did not cause the severe flooding; rather, it was the low elevation and the failing levee system *combined* with the erosion of the bayous—Louisiana's marshes and bogs that had protected the city in the past—that in the final analysis did the city in. The Great Swamp, like the southern bayous, acts as a giant sponge soaking up excess water and thereby lessening or preventing floods in nearby, generally more populated areas.

Directions to Green Chimneys:
Take I-684. When it ends at SR-22, go straight, continuing another 3.5 miles. Turn right onto Doansburg Road (CR-65). (Or, take I-84 to exit 18, SR-311 North towards Patterson. After a little more than a mile, SR-311 intersects with SR-164. Bear right onto SR-164, staying on it for just over 3 miles, then turn right onto SR-22 South. At 2.7 miles turn left onto Doansburg Road.) After about a mile and a half you will start to see signs for Green Chimneys, a large complex offering a variety of services to children. The boat launch will be on your left, two miles from where you turned onto Doansburg Road.

The Paddle:

My husband Joe and I launched our kayaks there a few days after a rather heavy rainfall. The swamp, it seemed, was doing its job. The water level was high, at least a foot above the base of many of the trees that rose mystically as though from a lake.

We wanted to follow the East Branch of the Croton River northwards, but could not quite find the river. Water was everywhere, and so it was hard to figure out where to paddle. We had more success when we turned the kayaks around and headed south, finally locating the river by searching for the current, which was quite strong. Explore outside the current and there the still water of the swamp abounds with birds—the expected geese and mallards, red-winged blackbirds and sandpipers, and the less common wood ducks and herons. Continuing to tack back and forth with the current, we proceeded slowly southward and after a mile or so crossed under the Doansburg Road bridge.

Coming to a place where the current picked up, we wondered whether we would be able to make it back to our starting point. I waited by the edge as the current swept Joe's kayak over some rocks and down a slight drop. He surged forward, turned the kayak around and, paddling hard and deep, barreled back towards me. He had done it, and so we decided to travel on.

Much of the contiguous land is privately owned. A few houses, occasional docks, and even a horse in a corral bordered the banks I passed. I quickly discerned that this section of the Great Swamp lacked the totally wild feel of protected reserves. Yet, unlike many of the rivers that had become major transportation routes during the eighteenth and nineteenth centuries including, of course, the Hudson and its tributaries, here there were no relics of a bygone era: no abandoned factories and no vacant warehouses. The Great Swamp is the backyard to many suburban homes, and that fact shows that we *can* live alongside of nature and safeguard it at the same time.

We returned to Green Chimneys in the fall when the water levels were not so high, and we were disappointed to find fallen trees and beaver dams repeatedly blocking the southward flow. So we chose instead to follow the course of the river, now contained within its banks, upstream as it switched back and forth leading into an open "lake" area framed by thinning, colorful foliage and small, rising mountains. Poking around,

▶ **East Branch Croton River—Starting from Green Chimneys**

I spotted a muskrat that swam to a massive root structure on the bank and hid in its intertwining shoots, and a kingfisher that flitted from branch to branch and screeched its muted, but raucous, rattle. Though many of the migratory birds had left for the south, the thinning foliage allowed for excellent wildlife viewing.

Helpful Web site:

- http://www.frogs-ny.org/index.html
  is the home site of Friends of the Great Swamp (FrOGS), an organization whose mission is the preservation of the swamp. This site offers in-depth scientific information about the biodiversity that typifies this area, including information about the watershed itself, the flora and the fauna. The site lists access points to the swamp and gives information about its history, lore, upcoming events, and recreational opportunities.

The Great Swamp absorbs much of the excess rainfall
and provides a habitat to untold wildlife.

P-3   East Branch Croton River from Patterson to Green Chimneys—*Mica and Beaver Dams*

- **Route:** Put in at the Patterson Environmental Park. Paddle south going under State Route 22 (SR-22) overpass and on down to Green Chimneys access.
- **Total Mileage:** Just under 6 miles one way. (May be done as an up to 12-mile round trip.)
- **Difficulty:** Moderate. **L P O** (See page 18.)
- **Setting:** Swamp forest, floodplain forest.
- **Hazards:** Watch for poison ivy attached to overhanging branches and surrounding you when portaging. It grows extensively in the swamp.
- **Remarks:** Requires two vehicles if done as a one-way trip. Both beaver dams and low-hanging branches will likely necessitate some portages, depending on water levels. Plant growth may impede progress between SR-22 overpass and Green Chimneys during mid- to late-summer months.

Directions to Green Chimneys:

Take I-684. When it ends at SR-22, go straight, continuing another 3.5 miles. Turn right onto County Route 65 (CR-65), also called Doansburg Road. (Or, take I-84 to exit 18, SR-311 North towards Patterson. After a little more than a mile, SR-311 intersects with SR-164. Bear right onto Route 164, staying on it for just over 3 miles, then turn right onto SR-22 South. At 2.7 miles turn left onto Doansburg Road.) After about a mile and a half you will start to see signs for Green Chimneys, a large complex offering a variety of services to children. Parking for river access will be on your left, two miles from where you turned onto Doansburg Road. Leave one vehicle here.

Directions from Green Chimneys to the Patterson Environmental Park:

Leaving the parking lot, turn left and stay on CR-65 (East Branch Road) until it ends after a little over 2 miles. Turn left onto Haviland Hollow Road (CR-68) and right onto SR-22 North for 2.3 miles. Turn left on SR-311 and go into the hamlet of Patterson. Go 0.8 mile, then turn left onto South Street. The park is on Marble Quarry Road. Turn left and cross the railroad tracks. You can launch your boat into the river at the end of the dirt road.

▶ **East Branch Croton River from Patterson to Green Chimneys**

P-3 East Branch Croton River from Patterson to Green Chimneys

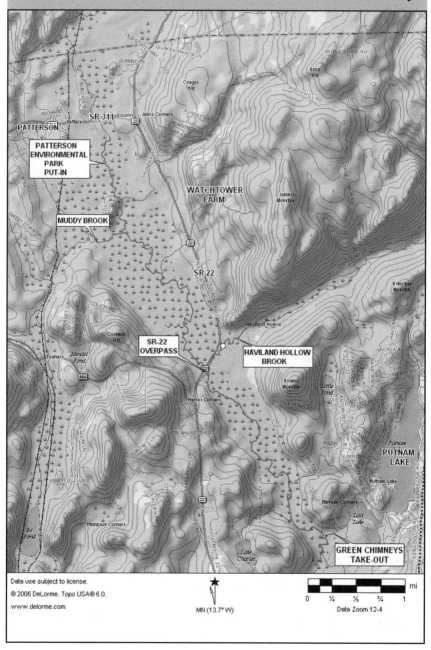

The Paddle:

Friends of the Great Swamp offers several guided canoe trips of the area. To explore this part of the river, I joined an all-day ecological safari led by environmentalist Jim Utter, a professor at SUNY Purchase and founder and chairman of FrOGS. He offered a wealth of information about the birds—identifying, by their calls, vireos, woodpeckers, and wrens—the plant life—pointing out the native duck potato, lizard's tail, and smart-weed—the geology—explaining the formation of the floodplains, the function of the wetlands, and the significance of the minerals found in the water. Though I might not remember all of the specifics of what Jim shared with us during the trip, he certainly impressed me with the importance of the swamp and its biodiversity, and the urgency of pro-tecting it and our other wetlands.

Leaving the launch area in Patterson, I was immediately struck by the contrast between this section of the river and the course south of Green Chimneys. On our left, posted signs adorning the trees indicated that this was county land; on our right, town land. The intrusion of subur-bia, the force of people pushing into and irrevocably changing the water-shed, is certainly less apparent here. We meandered through a dense swamp forest with its multiple levels of foliage: red maples and other hardwood trees grow tall, providing shade for an understory of shrubs; yellow irises rise flowering in clumps, their spiked leaves surrounded by smartweed, the dominant water plant. Though after a day of rain the water levels were high for early June, the current seemed slack. Here the low banks allow any overflow to spread out, decreasing the forward flow of the river.

We leisurely followed the river south, turning our kayaks and canoes sharply with its bends. Jim Utter pointed out the constant changes in the wetland. The roots of trees that have adapted to the high water content of the soil build extensive structures—wide but very shallow. Such trees easily topple over. The resulting deadfall sometimes impedes progress down the river. Fortunately for us, the fallen trees were off to the sides. Their main trunks were dead, but their roots were still alive, supporting what had been limbs, now transformed into trees. The vista opened up somewhat to the east, and in the distance through the trees we could make out the Watchtower Farm. Jim pointed out that agricul-ture has historically posed a threat to the watershed through the use

▶ **East Branch Croton River from Patterson to Green Chimneys**

On a guided wildlife safari, kayakers and canoers follow the flow
of the East Branch of the Croton River southward.

of pesticides and fertilizers, which ultimately drain into the rivers and
pollute the water. On our right the Muddy Brook, dividing into slight
and twisting channels, fed in to the East Branch. Then, after a little over
three miles of snaking through the swamp, we reached the SR-22 overpass, where a lunch of wraps and homemade desserts awaited us.

If you choose to stop here—it is another possible launch site—take
care. To the northeast, just beneath the bridge, lies a stagnant pool, a perfect breeding place for mosquitoes. In fact, despite my original concern
about bugs when I started kayaking, this was one of the only times they
actually caused a problem. Not only do you need to dodge the biting
insects, but you should watch out for poison ivy as well. It grows well in
the swamp, and there is quite a lot on the bank leading from the overpass down to the water.

Well fed and back in the river once more, we turned off to the right to
explore the mouth of the Haviland Hollow Brook. The water in this small
tributary is clear—according to Jim, the brook is used as a standard for

clean water—and you can see its sandy bottom studded with sparkling pieces of mica, a result of erosion from the low mountains in eastern New York and Connecticut through which the brook flows. In the lead now and low in my kayak, I ducked under a branch crossing the stream. The canoes, not quite so maneuverable, were blocked. When I turned around to go back, I noticed thick ropes of poison ivy twisting around the branch. Crouching low again, I steered underneath, but the current kept turning the boat and pushing me towards the vine. After several attempts I made it under and vowed to stay more alert.

Back on the East Branch, the scenery changed somewhat. With the additional water of the two feeder streams, Muddy Brook and Haviland Hollow Brook, the current picked up noticeably. The increased current in the river dug out a deeper channel into the swamp. The banks on either side seemed built up, containing the water inside the channel and not allowing any possible floodwaters to spread out, thus further increasing the current. The river here turns and twists around bends created and accentuated by the current, eroding one bank and depositing silt and sediment on the other. Huge construction projects of beaver lie adjacent to the river. Muskrats and otters as well as beaver populate the swamp, but our five canoes and two kayaks must have warned them away. Despite our presence, though, the place teemed with birds. Redwinged blackbirds flashed their yellow and red epaulets, great blue herons glided overhead, geese took off and circled, and a pair of kingbirds chased each other, the male displaying his colorful tail feathers.

As we continued south we crossed several beaver dams. Because of the recent rains, we were able to paddle over most of them. Two or three times, however, we had to portage around them, lifting or dragging our boats to avoid the obstacles. Finally the scenery opened up: the river spread out flat, lake-like; the vegetation thinned; the shrubs disappeared. Trees on the banks were silhouetted against the white sky, and low mountains were visible in the distance. A few more turns, and just under three miles from where we had had lunch, we pulled our canoes and kayaks ashore at the Green Chimneys access.

This trip through the Great Swamp heightened my awareness of just what a tenuous treasure our wetlands are. Industry once was the major threat to our waterways, damming them to provide power, then dumping into them pollutants and waste. Agriculture still threatens our water

▶ **East Branch Croton River from Patterson to Green Chimneys**

with chemicals that wash into our rivers and streams. But land development associated with sprawl may pose the greatest threat of all to the wetlands. Like farmers in the past, developers today want to drain our wetlands in an attempt to reclaim land.

Helpful Web site:
• http://www.frogs-ny.org/index.html
  is the home site of Friends of the Great Swamp (FrOGS), an organization whose mission is the preservation of the swamp. This site offers in-depth scientific information about the biodiversity that typifies this area including information about the watershed itself, the flora and the fauna. The site lists access points to the swamp and gives information about its history, lore, upcoming events, and recreational opportunities.

P-4– P-6 Putnam County Ponds and Lakes

P-4 Canopus Lake in Philipstown
(Clarence Fahnestock Memorial State Park)

- **How to get there:** Take the Taconic State Parkway to the exit for State Route 301 West. Continue for half a mile. The lake is on your right.
- **Where to put in:** Pass the park headquarters. You can launch from the rowboat rental area and park across the street, or continue another few hundred yards to a parking area adjacent to the lake.
- **Remarks:** A dam divides this scenic 103-acre lake. Boating is permitted in the southwestern half of the lake, the section adjacent to the road. To use your own boat, you need the New York State Taconic Region annual boat pass, which can be purchased at the park office or at the boathouse. No daily use fee is charged.

Web sites:
- http://nysparks.state.ny.us/parks/info.asp?parkId=129 gives information about the use of the park.

- http://www.dec.state.ny.us/website/dfwmr/fish/lakemaps/canplkmap. pdf offers a map of Canopus Lake. Though not meant for navigational use, the map gives water surface area, depths, contours, and species of fish found.

P-5 Stillwater Pond in Putnam Valley
(Clarence Fahnestock Memorial State Park)

- **How to get there:** The only way to get to the lake is via the Taconic State Parkway southbound. If you are going northbound, exit at State Route 301, and get on the Taconic, heading south. The chained entrance is at mile marker 29.6—a quick exit from the parkway.
- **Where to put in:** The parking area is on your left as you enter. A poorly maintained road descends to the lake. Despite signs stating no motorized vehicles should use the road, no-parking signs right by the lake suggest that boaters use the road for loading and unloading.

▶ **Putnam County Ponds and Lakes**

■ **Remarks:** The 55-acre lake seems very remote. Only the constant hum of cars on the parkway belies its isolation. To use your own boat, you must purchase the New York State Taconic Region annual boat pass. In addition you need a key, which the park office distributes for no additional charge. No daily use fee is charged.

Web sites:

• http://nysparks.state.ny.us/parks/info.asp?parkId=129 gives information about the use of the park.

• http://www.dec.state.ny.us/website/dfwmr/fish/lakemaps/stillpdmap. pdf offers a map of Stillwater Pond. Though not meant for navigational use, the map gives water surface area, depths, contours, and species of fish found.

P-6 White Pond in Kent

■ **How to get there:** Take the Taconic State Parkway to State Route 301 East. At 3.25 miles, SR-301 turns sharply to the right. Instead, go straight onto Farmers Mills Road (County Route 42). Go just over 2 miles, then bear left onto White Pond Road. The parking lot and launch area are .25 mile ahead on your right.

■ **Where to put in:** From the parking lot, access is easy: a few steps down a gentle slope to the water's edge.

■ **Remarks:** This area is maintained by the DEC for the public free of charge. The 138-acre lake is bordered by woods—the state owns 267 acres of land surrounding the lake—with some marsh toward the south end.

Web site:

• http://www.dec.state.ny.us/website/dfwmr/fish/lakemaps/whitpdmap. pdf offers a map of White Pond. Though not meant for navigational use, the map gives water surface area, depths, contours, and species of fish found.

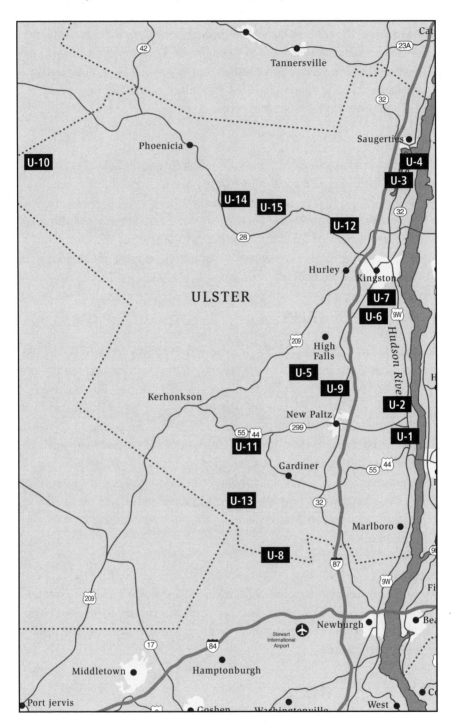

4

Ulster County

"So-this-is-a-River."

"THE River," corrected the Rat.

"And you really live by the river? What a jolly life!"

"By it and with it and on it and in it," said the Rat. "It's brother and sister to me, and aunts, and company, and food and drink, and (naturally) washing. It's my world, and I don't want any other. What it hasn't got is not worth having, and what it doesn't know is not worth knowing."

---

from *Wind in the Willows* by Kenneth Grahame

| U-1 | **Black Creek in Lloyd**
—The Mystery of Swamps |

- **Route:** From New Paltz Road in the town of Lloyd, travel northward as Black Creek winds through swamps and woodlands, crosses State Route 299 and heads towards Chodikee Lake.
- **Total Mileage:** Approximately 5 miles round trip.
- **Difficulty:** Easy.
- **Setting:** Swamps and woodlands.
- **Hazards:** None.
- **Remarks:** Logs, beaver dams, and extreme shallows often seasonally block course or necessitate brief portaging. Rocks and changes of elevation with small waterfalls prevent access to either Chodikee Lake to the north or Lake Sunset to the south.

Black Creek meanders through an area in Ulster County currently under great pressure to develop. Strip malls and storage facilities, like invasive weeds, now sprout along the State Route 299 (SR-299) corridor, the main route from the New York State Thruway to Poughkeepsie and other Dutchess County points. Yet only feet away from the rush and horns of semis and SUVs and in stark contrast to them lies a pristine area, home to a diversity of wildlife, a place where turtles, snakes, herons, muskrats, and beaver abound.

Directions:
From exit 18 on the New York State Thruway, head east toward Poughkeepsie for 2.6 miles. Make a right onto New Paltz Road (County Route 12). Continue for one and a quarter miles until New Paltz Road passes over Black Creek, which is clearly marked by DEC signs. You can pull your vehicle off on the right and walk down a rather steep bank to launch.

The Paddle:
From here you can explore the creek heading south for about a quarter of a mile. Go around a bend or two and you will see what appears to be a small earthen dam holding back a pool of water a couple of feet above you. With not too much difficulty you can pull your boat out on the left and put in again above the dam. Continue south. When the trees have no

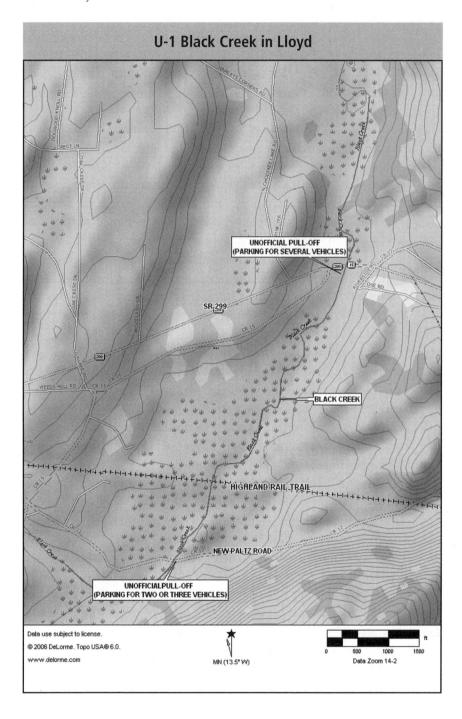

U-1 Black Creek in Lloyd

leaves, above you on your right you can make out a few houses and the road from which you launched. In this area, rarely traversed by kayakers, you are likely to scare up nesting waders. A couple of hundred feet later and the creek becomes impassable with its shallows, rocks and elevation changes. Return to where you parked.

Go under the New Paltz Road overpass and head north. You paddle, making one sharp turn after another, under the Highland Rail Trail, out of woodlands and into a swampy area. Leave behind the wood thrushes and listen to the songbirds of the fields. You may notice that several of the now sparser trees are dead, some standing almost in defiance of the laws of physics, their huge trunks whittled down to pencil points. This is the work of industrious beavers—and a warning of possible obstructions ahead. In this area you may have to negotiate a variety of obstacles, depending on the season and whether other kayakers have graciously cleared the creek. There are beaver dams, logs jammed between the narrow shores, and dense foliage. But unless the water levels are very low, the obstructions are negotiable and pushing through is well worth the effort. Glancing behind, you see Illinois Mountain—clearly identifiable by an obtrusive radio antenna—one of several hills and bluffs that dot the western shore of the Hudson River.

Black Creek is so dark—hence its name—from its bottom having filled with tannic acid from the hemlocks on the shoreline, and so narrow that in places overhanging branches touch trees on the opposing shore. It suggests an exotic place, a distant time. Only the antenna on Illinois Mountain belies the wilderness feel and timelessness of the spot. The sounds are the sounds of the wilds—birds call, frogs croak—until you round a bend and approach the SR-299 overpass a little over a mile from where you started. Suddenly civilization, loud and alien, assails you. There, on your left, is an alternate boat-launch site exactly four miles east of Thruway exit 18. If you choose to enter the creek here, pull off shortly after passing Chodikee Lake Road on your left. The grassy area just before South Riverside Road on your right offers parking and relatively easy access to the creek.

Crossing under the state road and proceeding north, you notice that the creek has widened and the ecology has changed. Woodlands flank the shore to your left; outcroppings of rock line the other shore. Leaving these rocks behind, look for an active beaver lodge off to your

▶ **Black Creek in Lloyd**

right. Once again you are paddling through swamp. After about three-quarters of a mile, the creek splits. Go straight and you will paddle into a dead-end bog of warm, rather stagnant water teeming with fish, frogs and insects. Black Creek veers off to the left, no longer navigable, as it drops over rocks and makes its way toward Chodikee Lake.

On the edge of Black Creek, home to abundant wildlife, a northern water snake suns itself.

U-2 Chodikee Lake in Highland
—Beaver Dams and Nesting Herons

- **Route:** Head north from boat launch toward outlet into Black Creek. Stop to observe heron rookery. Follow Black Creek to waterfall.
- **Total Mileage:** 3 miles roundtrip.
- **Difficulty:** Easy.
- **Setting:** Thin woods, marsh.
- **Hazards:** None.
- **Remarks:** Low water levels, fallen logs, and plant growth may impede progress somewhat during late summer months.

Winding and turning, Black Creek flows into the 63-acre Chodikee Lake in the town of Lloyd before continuing its northward course five miles to the Hudson River. The Highland Residential Center sits on the east bank of the lake. Though its sign indicates rather euphemistically that the facility is under the purview of New York's Children and Family Services, the layers of razor wire around its perimeter reveal the harsher truth. On the west side, a dock extends into the lake. From the water this is the only visible sign of a summer camp. The rest of the lake is untamed and protected by the DEC rule prohibiting gasoline-powered boats. It is a haven for birds and beaver, a paradise for birdwatchers, fishermen, and kayakers.

Directions:
Get off the New York State Thruway in New Paltz at exit 18. Turn right onto State Route 299 (SR-299), heading east towards Poughkeepsie. Continue for four miles, then turn left onto Chodikee Lake Road. Bear left where the road splits after a mile; the right fork heads to the state facility. One more mile, and you should spot a DEC sign on the left side of the road. The turn in for the lake, however, is on your right. If you miss the entrance to the lake access, you will see clusters of cabins from the camp. A little further and Chodikee Lake Road dead-ends.

The Paddle:
This launch site provides plenty of parking. You can back your car down to the water, a narrow channel that leads into Chodikee, and unload.

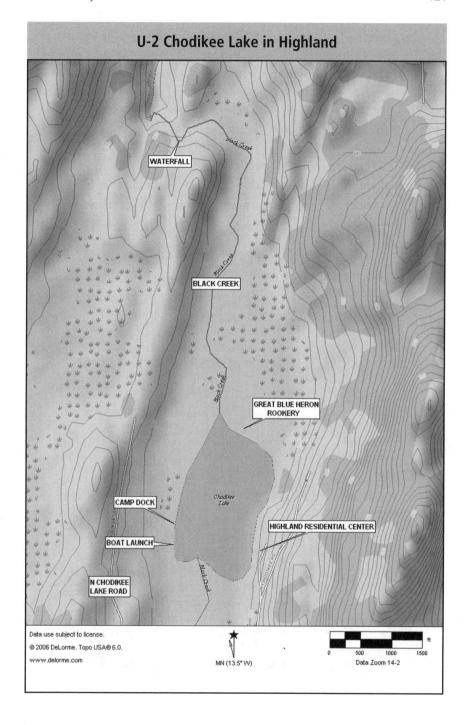

U-2 Chodikee Lake in Highland

WATERFALL

Black Creek

BLACK CREEK

GREAT BLUE HERON
ROOKERY

Chodikee
Lake

CAMP DOCK

HIGHLAND RESIDENTIAL CENTER

BOAT LAUNCH

N CHODIKEE
LAKE ROAD

Data use subject to license.

© 2006 DeLorme. Topo USA® 6.0.

www.delorme.com

MN (13.5° W)

0   500   1000   1500   ft

Data Zoom 14-2

Marsh grasses and shrubs, ringed by rather thin and young woods, border the lake. Paddle in and go to your left, passing the dock from the camp. Ahead on the shore you will notice a number of standing dead trees. Whether the result of a parasite, blight, beaver activity, or flooding, these snags are the hallmark of this section of Black Creek. As you approach the northern edge of the lake, look for the large treetop nests of the great blue heron. Here they breed in the spring, safe from the intrusion of man and machine.

Protective of their young, the birds are especially skittish in the spring, so proceed slowly and quietly. If you watch long and carefully, you may well be rewarded with a view of the large birds feeding their big babies.

Find the outlet back into Black Creek to your left on the northwestern side of the lake. Follow the flow of the creek as it zigzags back and forth around bends. You can explore small side tributaries depending on the time of year, the amount of plant growth, and the level of the water,

Great blue heron rookery at Chodikee Lake: a baby pokes its head
out of its nest as it awaits its mother and food.

▶ Chodikee Lake in Highland

Beaver lodges dot the edges of the Black Creek outlet from Chodikee.

perhaps flushing out a pair of swans or mallards. Several beaver lodges, some of them huge construction projects, lie adjacent to the shores.

Turtles sunning themselves on logs, sticks, and rocks protruding from the surface of the water flop into the water as they hear the approaching boat. Frogs jump off the huge leaves of water lilies. Removed from both houses and industry, the place is quiet. A mile past the lake, you hear the waterfall before you see it. The vegetation changes dramatically: the marsh and snags are gone, the woods are denser. Pull up onto the shore just before the creek turns to the right, plunging over the waterfall. The land, posted, belongs to the Township of Esopus Sportsmen's Club. Explore a little or have a snack before you head back.

In *Prose Works* (1892) Walt Whitman wrote about Black Creek. "[I]n a wild scene of woods and hills ... we have come to visit a waterfall. I never saw finer or more copious hemlocks, many of them large, some old and hoary ... Enveloping all, the monotone and liquid gurgle from the hoarse impetuous copious fall—the greenish-tawny, darkly transparent waters, plunging with velocity down the rocks, with patches of milk-white foam—a stream of hurrying amber, thirty feet wide, risen far back in the hills and woods, now rushing with volume—every hundred rods a fall, and sometimes three or four in that distance. A primitive forest, druidical, solitary and savage—not ten visitors a year—broken rocks everywhere—shade overhead, thick underfoot with leaves—a just palpable wild and delicate aroma."

This trip is short and easy and although the forest is no longer either so "solitary" or so "primitive," the place is a gem and promises to be even better in the future. By state law, wetlands are now better protected than ever, precluding additional development on the banks of the lake. According to the Town of Lloyd Environmental Conservation Council, plans are in the works to extend the watercourse through a series of land trails and portages that will link the Black Creek route south of SR-299 to Chodikee Lake and enable kayakers to continue all the way to the Hudson River.

Helpful Web site:

• http://www.dec.state.ny.us/website/dfwmr/fish/lakemaps/chodlkmap. pdf offers a map of Chodikee Lake. Though not meant for navigational use, the map gives water surface area, depth, contours, and species of fish found.

▶ **Chodikee Lake in Highland**

Esopus Creek from the Village of Saugerties towards Kingston
—Village, Cliffs, and a Nature Preserve

U-3

- ■ **Route:** From the Saugerties Village Beach, follow the creek westward, away from the center of the village around a ninety-degree bend to the south as it heads towards the city of Kingston, until the creek narrows into rapids.
- ■ **Total Mileage:** Just under 5 miles round trip.
- ■ **Difficulty:** Easy to moderate. **CH** (See page 18.)
- ■ **Setting:** Woods and houses visible on north/west side of creek; south/east bank, woods and escarpment.
- ■ **Hazards:** None.
- ■ **Remarks:** Near the village of Saugerties, the Esopus is deep, allowing for paddling in any season. Strong winds can churn up the creek.

Directions:

To follow the Esopus away from the Hudson, park your car at the Saugerties Village Beach. After exiting the Thruway at Saugerties (exit 20), stay on State Route 32 (SR-32) as it makes several turns. Eventually the route turns right from Main Street onto Partition Street, where SR-32 joins up with US-9W. Continue for 0.4 mile until you see the bridge that crosses the creek. Routes 32 and 9W turn left onto the bridge. You should instead stay on Partition Street, which ends about three hundred feet ahead at a small, sandy beach with plenty of parking and a boat ramp providing for an easy launch.

The Paddle:

Turn right and you will find yourself in a wide body of water, more a river than a creek, a far cry from the shallow rapids that have imbued the Esopus with its local reputation as an exciting whitewater run. The river-like terrain here is possibly a result of the creation of the Partition Street dam in the early nineteenth century. Here the Esopus flows deep and is sometimes choppy, that is if a stiff wind stirs up small waves. On your right the village eventually recedes as you paddle by a handful of waterfront houses. They face the Esopus Bend Nature Preserve, a forever-wild acquisition of the Esopus Creek Conservancy, formed in 2003. If you hug the left bank, you will notice small streams, inlets into the creek.

U-3 Esopus Creek from the Village of Saugerties towards Kingston

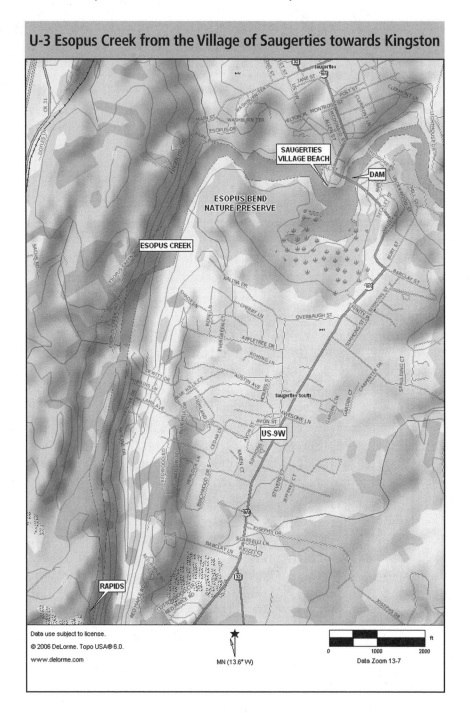

▶ **Esopus Creek from the Village of Saugerties towards Kingston**

Near their mouths they have deposited piles of silt, underwater sand hills that scrape the bottom of your boat, a miniature replication of a delta. Here, along the bank, you can find places to pull ashore and enjoy lunch or a hike. The preserve itself is rustic; the woods, with trails looping through them, support a great variety of wildlife. As you continue on, the scenery becomes more rugged, the woods eventually giving way to sheer cliff dropping precipitously to the water's edge. The houses on the right bank at last give way to forest, and up ahead the creek narrows. You can continue for a few hundred feet as the banks come closer, the creek becomes shallower, and more underwater rocks protrude. At some point you will have to give up your fight against the current and begin your return trip.

U-4 The Mouth of the Esopus Creek in Saugerties
—To the Lighthouse

- **Route:** From Waterfront Park in the village of Saugerties, go west to the dam; then, go back, pass the park and continue to the lighthouse, the point where the Esopus meets the Hudson.
- **Total Mileage:** 3 miles round trip.
- **Difficulty:** Moderate. **CH C** (See page 18.)
- **Setting:** Trees, houses visible along the shoreline, the mouth of the Esopus opening into the Hudson River.
- **Hazards:** Currents, tides, weather conditions, and boat traffic on the Hudson always pose some danger to small craft.
- **Remarks:** A little paddle with a lot of history.

The Esopus Creek begins on Slide Mountain, the tallest peak in the Catskills, dumps into the Ashokan Reservoir, part of the New York City Watershed, and then runs its circuitous course through a number of Ulster County towns, gradually heading eastward where it meets the Hudson River in the village of Saugerties. The creek is famous locally for a ten or so mile stretch of white water near the town of Phoenicia. The town profits from regular releases of water from the Schoharie Reservoir via the Shandaken Tunnel leading into the Esopus in the warm months, attracting tubers and kayakers who challenge its moderate rapids. As it flows eastward the creek broadens and the water becomes flat. In Saugerties, just south of the hub of the village, two places offer easy access to the creek. Waterfront Park allows for a short trip that can incorporate a tour of the renovated Saugerties Lighthouse.

Directions:
To get to the village of Saugerties, take the Thruway to exit 20. At the light at the end of the exit, turn right onto State Route 32 (SR-32) South and head east. Follow the state road for a mile as it turns, making first a right onto Market, then a left onto Main. Go one block. Turn right onto US-9W, Partition Street. Continue for half a mile until you come to an "erector-set" type of bridge. This bridge crosses the top of the dam and the Esopus. Immediately after the bridge turn left onto East Bridge Road. Waterfront Park is on your left directly after The Mill, an apartment complex. The park provides ample parking.

▶ **The Mouth of the Esopus Creek in Saugerties**

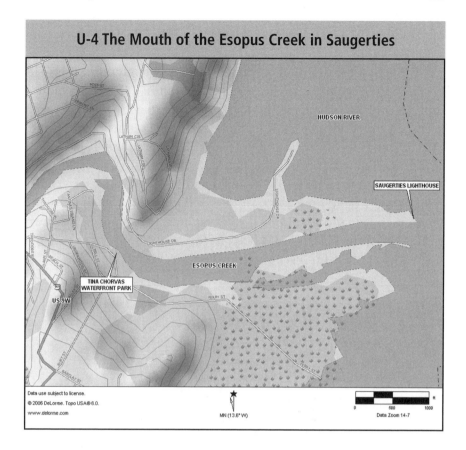

U-4 The Mouth of the Esopus Creek in Saugerties

The Paddle:

Put in your boat and head left. You can paddle around the bend a little over half a mile. You will find yourself beneath the bridge you crossed on US-9W, at the base of the Partition Street dam, a dam that in the nineteenth century powered Ulster Iron Works and a succession of paper mills. Turn back. Passing Waterfront Park, head east towards the mouth of the Esopus. This, too, is a short paddle; the Esopus empties into the Hudson a mile and half from the dam. On your left you will pass a number of houses and a Coast Guard station before you leave behind the density of the village. Now the houses drop away and you parallel a half-mile foot trail to the lighthouse. The Saugerties Lighthouse sits on a point of land precisely where the creek and river meet. From here you can attempt to either navigate the tidal and sometimes rough waters of the Hudson or, depending on currents and tides, dock or beach your kayak for a short visit to the lighthouse.

The lighthouse was originally built in 1838 when shipping was in its heyday and Saugerties was a major port. Rebuilt in 1869, it functioned until the mid-1950s when technological advances made lighthouses with keepers a thing of the past. It was essentially abandoned and fell into disrepair until the formation of the Saugerties Lighthouse Conservancy, whose mission to reconstruct the lighthouse was realized in 1990. Now, funded in part through its use as a bed and breakfast, the Conservancy maintains the lighthouse as a historical building with a small museum. On weekend afternoons during the late spring and summer, if no one is staying there, the lighthouse is open to the public. Even when it is not open to the public, however, you can still walk around the grounds.

Once an important warning for shipping vessels, the Saugerties Lighthouse at the mouth of the Esopus now houses a small museum and guesthouse.

▶ The Mouth of the Esopus Creek in Saugerties

Rondout Creek in the High Falls Area
—West of the Shawangunks

U-5

Poring over a map of Ulster County in search of waterways for boating, I kept zeroing in on the Rondout, which winds and turns, practically bisecting the county. A Google search, however, of the Rondout plus key words associated with canoes, kayaks, and launches yielded little, and word-of-mouth inquiries yielded little more. I'd already paddled the course from Creek Locks north to the Hudson, but that thick blue line running from Accord through High Falls and Rosendale kept catching my eye. So Kendra and I packed the kayaks and headed over the mountain to Ellenville in search of a place to launch.

We passed Minnewaska State Park and, descending the steep State Route 44-55 down towards Kerhonkson, went over the Rondout. After turning south onto a rural road towards Wawarsing, we stopped a local. "You know any place around here you can put a boat into the creek?" I whispered my guess to Kendra, *not a chance*. The short, rotund man hobbled across the road and proved me wrong. In a heavy Ukrainian accent he explained that he had lost his canoe along with his house in a fire. Yes, yes, he would like to help us. "This is a beautiful place to kayak. You put in near the old bridge near Napanoch and can kayak two miles back to Kerhonkson. Or if you want a ten-mile stretch of wider and deeper water, you can go from Accord through Alligerville to High Falls."

We followed his directions and parked our car by a bridge just outside a run-down community of shacks and trailers. Filled with expectation we launched our boats into the shallow water and went with the current through some picturesque and rustic places where unfortunately no one has heard of *leave no trace*, and then through two or three rocky riffles—moving flat water, I'd heard them described—until after a mile of abusing our sensibilities and the bottoms of our kayaks, we decided to return. Easier said than done. Where the current was too strong, we wound up walking our kayaks and slipping on algae-covered rocks.

Though the Rondout traverses the county, and from Accord on runs broad, it also runs shallow. Depending on the time of year and the rainfall amounts, you can negotiate the Accord to High Falls section with no portaging. However, you can paddle between two and three scenic miles south of High Falls pretty much any time of year.

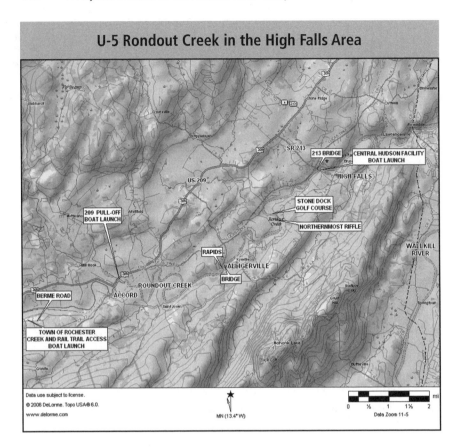

U-5 Rondout Creek in the High Falls Area

High Falls South

- ■ **Route:** South from State Route 213 in High Falls.
- ■ **Total Mileage:** 5 miles round trip.
- ■ **Setting:** Rural, hardwoods, occasional houses.
- ■ **Difficulty:** Easy.
- ■ **Hazards:** None.
- ■ **Remarks:** Some shallow areas with riffles at the southern end stop you from going further. In midsummer and drought conditions, the navigable portion of the creek will be shorter.

Directions from the south:

Exit the New York State Thruway in New Paltz (exit 18). Turn left onto State Route 299 (SR-299), also called Main Street, and go through the village, turning right onto SR-32 North. Continue for 7.4 miles, past the town of Tillson into Rosendale, and turn left at the light onto SR-213 West. Go 3.9 miles, passing the center of High Falls. Just before the intersection with County Route 1 (CR-1), also called Lucas Turnpike, and the SR-213 bridge over the creek, you will see a Central Hudson hydroelectric plant on your right. Pull into the parking area right before the intersection and the bridge. This area with parking and a ramp that allows for easy access to the Rondout is maintained jointly by Central Hudson and the High Falls Civic Association.

Directions from the north:
Exit the New York State Thruway at Kingston (exit 19). Bear right onto SR-28 West. Follow signs for US-209 South towards Ellenville. Continue on US-209 for 10 miles. Turn left onto SR-213. Go past CR-1 (1.3 miles). Cross the bridge over the Rondout. Pull into the parking lot by the hydroelectric plant on your left.

The Paddle:
The falls that has given the town its name is clearly marked with orange warning signs on your right as you launch. Turn left under the bridge. After less than a quarter of a mile, the creek turns slightly to the left, leaving the bridge no longer visible and the sounds of cars somewhat muted. For the first three-quarters of a mile or so, the creek is bounded on the right by Lucas Turnpike and by Berme Road on the left. The banks are fairly steep, however, and the roads are not generally seen from the water. At one point along here, the creek gets very shallow and some rocks protrude. If the season is dry, you may not be able to go any further. At another point the Rondout bends sharply to the right with Lucas Turnpike visible once more; there is actually a pull-off here for one or two cars by the side of the road and a place for an agile fisherman or kayaker to descend to the creek. After that first portion the road noise lifts and at last you feel the seclusion you have sought. Now you are likely to see the Canada geese, ducks, and swans that nest along the shores.

At last the creek turns sharply to the left and the scenery changes, becoming wilder. Ahead is an island, a perfect breeding ground for birds. Tree swallows skitter over the water's surface, red-winged blackbirds call out their warnings (perhaps of the approach of the kayak). On the left you see the edge of the Stone Dock Golf Course and, through the trees—if they do not yet have their foliage—the Mohonk Mountain House tower in the distance. Continue another quarter of a mile until you reach the northern-most riffle along the Accord to High Falls stretch of the Rondout. The current is too strong to paddle any further, so turn around and head back.

Accord to High Falls

- **Route:** From Accord northeast through Alligerville to High Falls.
- **Total Mileage:** 10.3 miles one way (with optional additional 3.5 miles if you put in from Berme Road).
- **Difficulty:** Challenging. **A R P O M** (See page 18.)
- **Setting:** Hardwood trees, farmland, occasional houses until the bridge in Alligerville; after the bridge, some dramatic rock outcroppings, some evergreen forests, hardwood forests, and occasional houses.
- **Hazards:** This is slow-moving flat water—occasional shallow riffles with rocks, very occasional small rapids. As with all moving water, caution must be taken.
- **Remarks:** Requires two vehicles—you will need to leave a second vehicle at the hydroelectric plant in High Falls. Most of the Rondout is rather shallow. When water levels are low, some portaging may be required. When extremely low, the creek may be impassable.

Directions from the Central Hudson parking lot to the Accord put-in:

Turn right onto State Route 213 (SR-213). At the light make a left onto County Route 1 (CR-1), also called Lucas Turnpike, which will end in six miles. Turn left onto SR-209. You are now approaching Accord. The town unfortunately does not provide easy access to the creek. You will pass a hardware store and a sign for a golf resort, both on your right. Look for a small bridge where the road crosses a stream just a little over a half mile from your turn onto SR-209. On the left side of the road is a pull-off with a dirt road leading down to a creek access with room for two or three vehicles, an access used primarily by fisherman. Launching from here is a bit tricky. You are parked between a stream on your left and the creek on your right. They join up a few hundred feet ahead. Getting into the kayak is easier on your left, but the stream is shallow and moving rapidly. You

▶ **Rondout Creek in the High Falls Area**

may need to portage a bit until the stream joins up with the Rondout. On your right the descent is rather steep and the bank is muddy. But once in the creek, the going is easy.

An alternative starting point is an official canoe and kayak access area maintained by the Town of Rochester off of Berme Road between Kerhonkson and Accord. This would add an additional three and a half miles to the trip.

The Paddle:
Rondout Creek meanders, turning first one direction, then another, coming alongside roads only occasionally. And even these roads—CR-1 and CR-6 —are not major throughways with heavy commercial traffic. This creates an idyllic setting for the ten-mile paddle, one relatively free of development. Farms, somewhat obscured by a tree line adjacent to the banks, alternate with woods. The water itself is flat for the most part, especially for the first two or three miles. After that, the creek becomes shallower from time to time, causing it to move faster. When water levels are high enough, you can run these riffles with little difficulty, occasionally scraping the rocks on the bottom. As you approach the bridge in Alligerville, the shallows become

Swimming between kayak and the Rondout shore, a swan considers flight.

more frequent, and finally you make a turn, glimpsing the bridge, just as you have to negotiate rapids with a comparatively strong current, the most challenging portion of this course. The water quiets down and you glide under the bridge, five and a half miles from where you put in.

The stretch from Alligerville to High Falls is more varied. Though there seems to be less agriculture, a submerged irrigation pump reveals the occasional farm. The few houses alongside the creek are larger and newer, a couple with decks overlooking the water. To your right you can catch an occasional glimpse of Sky Top Tower at the Mohonk Mountain House. I watched perplexed as a log with some green vegetation seemingly growing from it floated along by the creek edge, keeping pace with my kayak. The current was not strong, so I wondered how the log was moving so fast. Suddenly, a splash. The back of the "log" smacked the water, the front dove, and ripples circled outward at the mouth of a beaver lodge. The next time, I vowed, I would get a picture.

A little further and you will pass the golf course on your right. Shortly after this, Lucas Turnpike will approach the creek for the final time. Now the road noise and the sounds of people from the closer houses inform you that High Falls is nearby. A final turn to the right and you see the SR-213 bridge. Go under the bridge and to your right is the take-out.

▶ **Rondout Creek in the High Falls Area**

Rondout Creek in Eddyville
—Boulders and a Dam

U-6

- **Route:** From the DEC parking lot and boat launch in the town of Ulster north to the waterfall near the State Route 213 (SR-213) bridge; return passing the launch heading south towards Rosendale until the first rapids.
- **Total Mileage:** Approximately 4.5 miles round trip.
- **Difficulty:** Easy to moderate. **CH** (See page 18.)
- **Setting:** Woodlands interspersed with houses, with more development on the west side as Creek Locks Road runs beside the Rondout.
- **Hazards:** The Eddyville Dam to the north; to the south some large rocks under the surface.
- **Remarks:** This portion of the creek is wide and deep.

In Queens, where I grew up, we used the word "creek" pretty much interchangeably with "stream," and either one could designate a trickling brook or, more likely, a dry river bed. Here in Eddyville the Rondout Creek is wide, feeling much more like a river than a stream. To this day, when I put my kayak into the Esopus or the Rondout and see the expanse of the creek, the rolling surface of the choppy water, I am in awe.

The Rondout, like most of the creeks and *kills* that abound in the Hudson River Valley on the west side of the river, begins in the Catskill Mountains. It starts its descent to the Hudson on Rocky Mountain, winds southwest through western Ulster County, and dips into Sullivan County where it dumps into the Rondout Reservoir, part of the New York City water system. There it joins up with waters from the Delaware River watershed funneled in through the Neversink and Delaware aqueducts. From there the Rondout continues first briefly southeast, then northeast as it makes its way towards the Hudson River in the city of Kingston.

Like the Hudson and most of its larger tributaries, the Rondout is rich in history. During the heyday of the steam engine and water transportation, the creek and its adjacent canal system bustled with boats, business, and trade. The relative peace and comparative lack of development there today, especially viewed from the seat of a small boat, contrast with its past as the commercial hub of the Rondout-Kingston area. With houses easily visible on the west bank, this course, while not

U-6 Rondout Creek in Eddyville

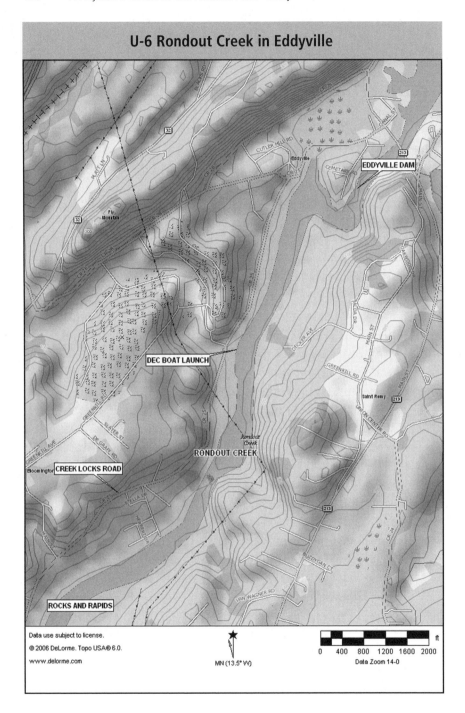

EDDYVILLE DAM

DEC BOAT LAUNCH

Rondout Creek

RONDOUT CREEK

CREEK LOCKS ROAD

Bloomington

ROCKS AND RAPIDS

Data use subject to license.

© 2006 DeLorme. Topo USA® 6.0.

www.delorme.com

MN (13.5° W)

0   400   800   1200   1600   2000   ft

Data Zoom 14-0

▶ **Rondout Creek in Eddyville**

wilderness, is a far cry from the flurry of activity that used to typify the Hudson and its tributaries.

The DEC built an access point to the Rondout on Creek Locks Road in the town of Ulster, a bit south of Kingston.

Directions from the south:

Take exit 18 off the New York State Thruway. Make a left turn onto SR-299 West into the village of New Paltz. Turn right onto SR-32 North and continue 7.4 miles to the intersection with County Route 25 (CR-25), also called Creek Locks Road, in Rosendale, just past the turnoff for SR-213 to High Falls. Turn right on Creek Locks, a rather curvy and hilly road. Look to your right and see the Rondout, at first shallow and rocky, then deeper and more navigable as you proceed. Drive 4.4 miles and you will find a clearly marked parking area with an easily negotiated descent to the creek itself.

Directions from the north:

Leave the Thruway at exit 19, Kingston. Follow the signs to I-587 (George Chandler Drive), which will end at a light after a little over a mile. Make an angled left turn onto Broadway, going for .4 mile. Turn right onto SR-32 South (Henry Street). Go .3 mile and turn left onto SR-213 for 2.7 miles. SR-213 will jog through this end of Kingston, left on Clinton Avenue, right on Greenkill Avenue, left on Wilbur Avenue, right on Dunn Street, all before turning right onto Abeel Street. Here, SR-213 picks up the Rondout Creek and you pass marinas and the remnants of a once-thriving waterfront. SR-213 will cross over the Rondout in Eddyville. Just before the bridge, turn right onto Creek Locks Road (CR-25). At .1 mile, Creek Locks Road bears left. Continue another .3 mile to the stop sign. The road to the right climbs steeply. Bear left, staying on Creek Locks Road and adjacent to the Rondout. Half a mile up, on the left, is the DEC access area.

The Paddle:

Turn your kayak left, going in the direction of the mouth of the Rondout and the Kingston waterfront. Ahead you see woods, for the creek makes a sharp turn—almost 180°—to the right. Continue around another bend, this time to the left. In front of you, trees overhanging the right bank

This sign, visible from the Rondout, serves as a clear reminder of the history of the region and the importance of the D&H, both the railroad and the canal.

partially obscure the Eddyville Bridge. The roar of falling water drowns out car engines, mowers, fishermen calling, the noises of civilization. You look around for the source of the sound, confused, until you realize your kayak is being pulled slowly but inexorably towards the flow toppling over the dam just a little under a mile from the parking lot. You have been paddling on a sort of shelf of water, the top of the falls hidden from view by the creek itself. It is time to turn around and head back.

Passing the beach where you first put in, keep paddling south. You will see the houses on Creek Locks Road on your right, and woods on the opposite side. As the road climbs, rock face forms the right bank as well, and the more populated area appears to give way to forest. The creek narrows somewhat, and in the middle of the creek several large rocks loom in the distance ahead. If you try paddling against the current, which picks up significantly as you approach the boulders, watch out for rocks just under the surface. This is as far as you can go in the Rosendale direction. Turn around and head back to the DEC launch.

► **Rondout Creek in Eddyville**

Rondout Creek in Kingston
—The Strand to the Dam

U-7

■ **Route:** Launching from the Strand in Kingston, paddle southwest to the Eddyville dam, then back.

■ **Total Mileage:** 6+ miles round trip.

■ **Difficulty:** Moderate. **CH C** (See page 18.)

■ **Setting:** Marina after marina masks the rather dramatic changes in scenery as you leave the Kingston riverfront with its restaurants, galleries, and shops and head towards Eddyville, a tiny hamlet halfway between Kingston and Rosendale.

■ **Hazards:** This trip begins at the point where the Rondout meets the Hudson. Tides, weather, and boat traffic always pose some danger to small craft.

■ **Remarks:** This trip combines human history and natural history, as well as urban and rural settings.

In an era when water transportation reigned supreme, Rondout's location at the midpoint on the Hudson River between New York City and Albany, and at the port of entry from the Rondout Creek and the Delaware and Hudson Canal, established its position as the principal port between the terminal cities. From the time the D&H Canal was completed in 1825 until the railway system supplanted the system of canals and waterways late in the century, Rondout was king, a commercial hub supplying the growing city ninety miles south with cement for bridges and roads, bluestone for sidewalks, Pennsylvania coal for fuel, and ice harvested during the winter months from the Hudson River for refrigeration in the hot summer months. With its nineteenth-century growth and economic prosperity, the village of Rondout joined with the village of Kingston, forming the incorporated city of Kingston. New technology, however, made much of the new city's commerce obsolete. The D&H Railroad replaced the canal. Quick-drying Portland cement dried up the demand for cement from Rosendale and other Ulster areas. Later the ice industry died, a victim of refrigeration. Like many other Hudson River ports, Kingston languished, the bustling activity of barges and tugboats a mere memory of its glorious past.

U-7 Rondout Creek in Kingston

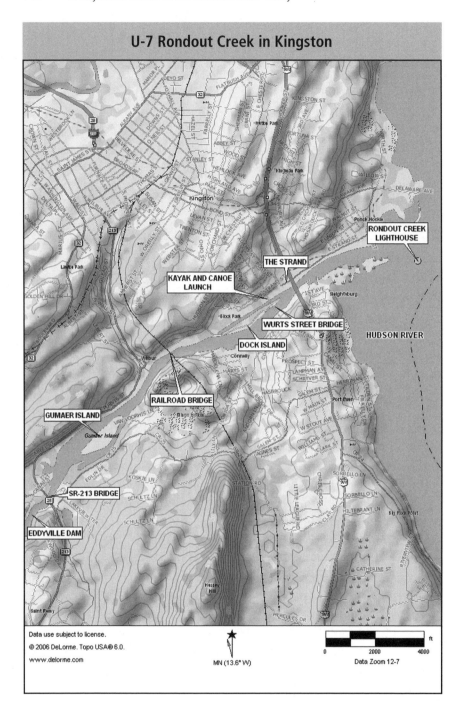

Data use subject to license.
© 2006 DeLorme. Topo USA® 6.0.
www.delorme.com

MN (13.6° W)

Data Zoom 12-7

▶ Rondout Creek in Kingston

Today, recreation and renovation have partially restored a portion of the river here. As you paddle from the Strand to the Eddyville dam, you pass marina after marina, your small kayak next to cabin cruisers, mega-yachts, trawlers, sailboats, and catamarans, clear indications of a brighter future for the port. Yet rusting hulls of partially submerged barges remain, vestiges of the city's past. These, too, you pass, as you head northeast towards the Hudson and the Rondout Creek Lighthouse.

Directions:

To get to the Kingston riverfront, take exit 19 from the New York State Thruway. At the traffic circle, turn onto I-587 (Chandler Drive). Get into the right lane. I-587 ends after a mile, at a traffic light. The left lane turns onto Albany Avenue. The right lane continues a couple of hundred feet, then turns left onto Broadway. Stay on Broadway past Kingston Hospital and Kingston High School, eventually leaving the business district. After 1.3 miles, take the left fork onto Lower Broadway. This takes you to the riverfront section of town called "the Strand." Turn right onto West Strand. The Rondout Creek is on your left with a number of public docks. The last of these docks, built low and close to the water, is intended for kayaks and other small boats. In addition to the easy access, there is plenty of parking.

The Paddle:

Across from you, as you put in, is Dock Island, a man-made spit of land created to provide both additional storage for the anthracite coal shipped via canal and river to New York City, and a place to deposit what was dredged from the bottom as the river was deepened to accommodate larger and larger boats. Despite its name, it is not an island and dead-ends a half a mile or so to the west. Turn to your left towards the Hudson—you will see the US-9W bridge over the Rondout ahead of you—and then right, around Dock Island and west upriver.

You go under the Wurts Street Suspension Bridge. Wurts Street was named, without a doubt, for one of the farsighted brothers who paid for the D&H Canal out of pocket, recognizing New York as a potential market for Pennsylvanian coal. On your right are the woods along the southern bank of Dock Island; on your left, Port Ewen; ahead, Wilbur Bridge, a still-used railroad crossing. You soon leave Dock Island behind, and

From the Rondout, a kayaker's view of the historic Kingston riverfront.

now the parade of marinas begins in earnest, hundreds and hundreds of boats anchored at their facilities. Fortunately, most of the Rondout is a no-wake zone, the designation allowing you to proceed safely. On the Port Ewen side huge, pyramid-like piles of what looks like gravel, and elaborate metal structures for conveying the material, serve as a reminder that the waterways and their banks are not simply for play.

Gumaer Island lies ahead, with the wider passage to the north. Just as you pass the last of the marinas and large boats, you glimpse the Eddyville Bridge ahead and hear the rumble of the water tumbling over the Eddyville dam. You may well see some fishermen by the water's edge. This is a favorite spot for anglers. Most species of fish cannot swim past the dam—a fact that has caused some sportsmen and environmentalists to advocate a renovation of the dam—and many fish congregate between the frothy waters beneath the dam and the SR-213 overpass.

Turning back towards Kingston three miles from where you started, explore the other side of Gumaer Island. Here there is no bustle, there are no boats, no bridges, and no buildings, and for the moment you feel far

▶ **Rondout Creek in Kingston**

from the urban experience of this Kingston paddle. This is a marsh, and in summer the vegetation grows lush. Around the island you re-emerge in the creek, which is so studded with boats that it seems busy even when they are all at anchor. If you stay to the right, you might notice the decaying wooden struts of some former structure. An array of plants is rooted in each, a hint that nature is again reclaiming the debris that we leave.

Approaching the Strand, you can turn left around Dock Island and return, or continue towards the Hudson to see the Rondout Creek Lighthouse. The mile stretch to the lighthouse is a stark reminder of what this port once was. Though Kosco oil tanks stand on both sides of the creek speaking of the energy of contemporary America, rusted barges and tugs, decaying planks and pilings, signal the death of another era. Tons of refuse and wreckage lie at the water's edge on the south bank.

Follow the waterway as it turns to the right and you will see at last the lighthouse, the third of three erected at the mouth of the Rondout Creek. This final rendition was built at the end of a long jetty and has withstood the hammering of the water and the weather since 1913. If the river is not too rough, you may be able to dock your kayak and look around before you head back to the small-boat launch at the Strand.

After your jaunt on the Rondout, enjoy the Kingston waterfront. Like some other Hudson River cities trying to encourage both tourism and the arts, Kingston has adopted a "First Saturday" program: galleries offer free admission and receptions throughout the city on the first Saturday of every month. So stop in to some of the galleries in the area, have lunch in one of the local restaurants, and visit the Hudson River Maritime Museum located at 50 Rondout Landing.

U-8 Wallkill River from Wallkill to Walden
—Crossing the County Line

In southern Ulster County and on into northern Orange County, a series of small rapids and dams impedes your progress on the Wallkill River. However, there are some navigable stretches that lend themselves to exploration in a kayak or canoe.

- **Route:** Putting in at the southern end of the village of Wallkill, go south towards Walden in Orange County; when returning, pass the boat launch and continue another quarter of a mile toward the bridge.
- **Total Mileage:** 4 miles round trip.
- **Difficulty:** Easy.
- **Setting:** The west side of the river is wooded and rustic, then gives way to fields and farmland; on the east side of the river a thin row of trees grows between the river and State Route 208 (SR-208).
- **Hazards:** Watch for the dam right before the bridge in Wallkill.
- **Remarks:** The river here is fairly shallow with riffles to the south. You could quite possibly portage around them and lengthen the trip.

SR-208, though a major north-south route, is for the most part a scenic road that twists and turns through several small Orange and Ulster county towns. Heading south on SR-208 from New Paltz, you can still look out across farmland and apple orchards and see beyond them the Shawangunks, the ridge line of a low but dramatic mountain range. You can also see the obtrusive buildings of the Wallkill Correctional Facility in stark contrast to the natural beauty of the area. Between the towns of Wallkill in Ulster County and Walden in Orange County, the road offers impressive views of the Wallkill River, and you can paddle this stretch of the river.

Directions:
From the New York State Thruway, take the Newburgh exit (exit 17) to SR-300 North, following the signs to I-84. Get onto I-84 West for about 9 miles. Take exit 5 and turn onto SR-208 North. Go right through the village of Walden. Watch for the small Town of Shawangunk Park on your left, just after the sheriff's substation, 6.8 miles from the intersection with I-84. Pull in. There is plenty of parking and easy access to the river.

▶ **Wallkill River from Wallkill to Walden**

U-8 Wallkill River from Wallkill to Walden

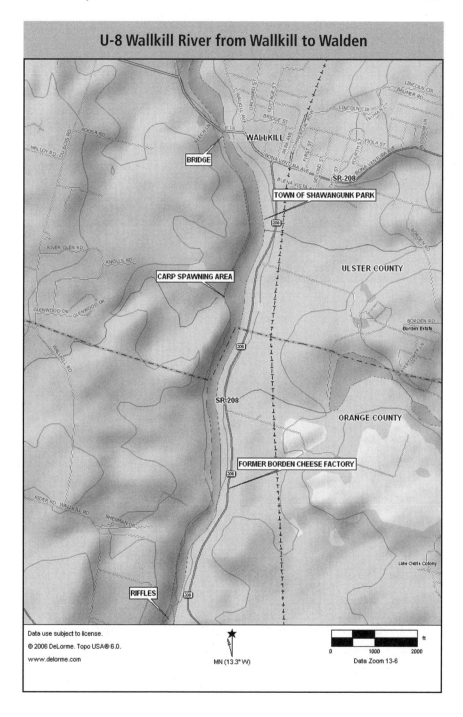

The Paddle:

When you put in your boat, notice the bridge over the river to your right. Shortly before the bridge is a dam, so your best bet is to turn left and head south. Some commercial buildings, including the police station you just passed on the road, are now visible on the east bank to your left. While as a driver the proximity of the river to the road offers the benefit of a scenic view, as a kayaker the nearness of the road is a drawback And so, after putting in, I immediately crossed the river to the far, and less developed, west bank. Down the river about a quarter of a mile, I noticed a pier next to a side channel. I turned in to explore the stream, which turned out to be shallow and not navigable beyond about a tenth of a mile. As I turned my kayak around, I was startled by a loud splash. I stayed quiet until I discovered the source—several two-foot-long brown fish swimming, jumping, and making the water murky. These, it turned out, were carp.

In spring, spawning carp churn up water in the Wallkill.

▶ **Wallkill River from Wallkill to Walden**

I quit the channel and turned right into a small area dotted with clumps of underwater plants, a carp spawning ground. Here I sat mesmerized by an early spring show of nature: splashing, jumping, pirouetting fish.

Continuing south, you leave the commercial buildings of the village of Wallkill behind. Around a turn the trees on the west side of the river disappear and give way to a panorama of fields and a large farmhouse. Trees partially block the state route on the east bank. Only the persistent hum of road noise serves as a reminder of civilization nearby. Then, through the foliage, you make out the hulk of an old, red-brick plant, the former Borden cheese factory, burned in a fire on March 19, 1997, but still standing. A little past that is a shallow and rocky area, a mini-rapids, but it is passable if water levels are sufficiently high. Go a little further and, unfortunately, just where SR-208 veers away from the river with the promise of a truly quiet and natural setting, you will encounter a rapids. Turn around and head back.

You can pass by the park where you launched and go about a quarter of a mile further towards the Bruyn Turnpike bridge, but be careful. Before the bridge and not clearly marked is one of the many dams that once powered this region. Head back to the park now, having glimpsed industry, nature, and agriculture in this one short trip.

U-9 Wallkill River from New Paltz to Rifton
—Eleven Miles of Almost Uninterrupted Paddling

- **Route:** From New Paltz to Sturgeon Pool.
- **Total Mileage:** Variable—allows for up to 17 miles round trip.
- **Difficulty:** Easy.
- **Setting:** Mainly woods, some farms, occasional houses and roads visible.
- **Hazards:** Dam in Rifton.
- **Remarks:** Several launches allow public access to the river at a number of points. You can paddle any of a number of sections of the 11-mile stretch of river between Sojourner Truth Park and Sturgeon Pool. Except in flood conditions, the northward current is slow, allowing for trips out and back.

It is natural that when I undertook writing this book, I began my explorations with the Wallkill River. Having lived in New Paltz for the past thirty years, I've become well aware of the Wallkill's wanderings. The flats north of New Paltz flood regularly. This is an annoyance to those of us who live west of the Wallkill and must rely on circuitous alternative routes home from town, but it is also an awesome reminder of the raw power of nature. Locals and tourists alike gather on the edge of the flooded areas with cameras and open mouths to gaze at the water, water everywhere, and to gawk at the occasional stranded car whose driver ignored the police warnings not to enter a flood zone, and whose car subsequently floated into the middle of a submerged corn field. Because of the Wallkill and its vagaries, I had needed to get national flood insurance on my first home on Springtown Road; if not, the bank would not have provided the mortgage.

The Wallkill begins its ninety-mile course in Sussex County, New Jersey, flows northward into Orange County in New York State and ends in Ulster County. There, in Rifton, a half a mile after leaving Sturgeon Pool, the Wallkill meets the Rondout Creek, which continues another seven miles until it finally feeds into the Hudson River in the city of Kingston a little past the city's recently renovated waterfront. The Wallkill is known not only for its supposedly unusual northward flow and its flooding, but also for its route through the Wallkill River National Wildlife Refuge on the New York/New Jersey state line. The refuge maintains three canoe access sites allowing for observation of the habitats that the

U-9 Wallkill River from New Paltz to Rifton

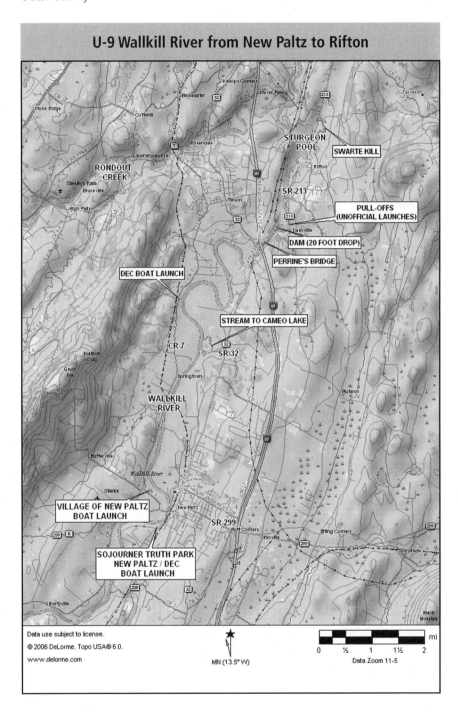

Data use subject to license.

© 2006 DeLorme. Topo USA® 6.0.

www.delorme.com

MN (13.5° W)

0   ½   1   1½   2   mi

Data Zoom 11-5

refuge protects: floodplain forests and wet meadows. Most of the refuge itself lies south of the state border in New Jersey.

Further north, in Ulster County, over the last few years state and local governments have constructed several boat launch sites on the Wallkill. Some are usable only seasonally, depending on the amount of rainfall. (While the Wallkill floods are famous, much of the river is wide, shallow, and rocky.) The four launch sites shown on the map all lead to stretches of the river passable even with little rainfall and in drought conditions. You can use any of these river accesses and create a trip of whatever length you desire. The Wallkill is quiet water here, and you can kayak in both directions.

Directions to Sojourner Truth Park:

Take I-87 to exit 18, New Paltz. Turn left onto State Route 299 (SR-299), also called Main Street. To get to the southernmost of these launches, follow SR-299 through the Village of New Paltz for 1.5 miles. Turn left onto Water Street. The road winds around behind the Water Street Market. You will come to a four-way stop. Continue straight (do not go up the hill) onto Plains Road. Less than half a mile on the right is the parking area for Sojourner Truth Park. There the Village of New Paltz and the New York State Department of Environmental Conservation jointly maintain a small-boat and fishing access, and a parking area for several cars.

Directions to Springtown Road boat launch in New Paltz:

From the New Paltz exit on I-87, turn left onto SR-299 West. Continue through the village of New Paltz for 1.7 miles. Immediately after the bridge over the Wallkill River, turn right onto Springtown Road. Less than a quarter of a mile up the road and before the fork leading to Mohonk, pull off on the right. You can pull your car close to the river and unload. There is plenty of parking.

Directions to Springtown Road boat launch in Rosendale:

The DEC constructed a boat launch about four miles north of New Paltz. To get there, make the right turn onto Springtown Road as above. At the fork, bear right and continue on Springtown Road approximately 3.6 miles. A sign clearly shows the pull-off on the right. Severe flooding in the spring of 2005 washed away the original wooden launch, but the DEC rebuilt it, this time sturdier.

▶ **Wallkill River from New Paltz to Rifton**

Directions to SR-213 river access:

North of the dam there are no other maintained boat launches. However, as you drive along Route 213 you will see several places to pull off and park a car. Some of them are accessible to the river. Use your judgment. You can get to SR-213 by turning onto SR-32 North out of New Paltz. Just shy of five miles north of town, turn right on SR-213. (Alternatively, if you are starting from Springtown Road, continue north. Make a right onto River Road, which was recently reopened after being shut down for years while the Army Corps of Engineers fixed a serious erosion problem where the road comes extremely close to the Wallkill. River Road ends at SR-32. Make a right, cross the bridge over the river, and then take your next left on SR-213.) You will see Perrine's Bridge on your left, and Woodcrest, the Bruderhof community, on your right. Keep going. The dam is visible from the road. After you pass the dam keep a lookout for a place to pull off.

The Paddle:

Although from Sojourner Truth Park you cannot go far in a southward direction, a leisurely paddle south will afford some impressive views of both the Faculty Towers at SUNY New Paltz and Sky Top Tower at the Mohonk Mountain House. A northern route offers several miles of unobstructed paddling. About a quarter of a mile north of the launch, you will pass under SR-299. Go another half a mile and you will see the Springtown Road boat launch in New Paltz.

Navigating north from here, you paddle through both woods and farms. About 1.75 miles ahead you will see the old railroad bridge. It is a landmark on the rail trail, a linear park maintained by the Wallkill Valley

Tower at Mohonk viewed from the Wallkill River.

Rail Trail Association, on what was formerly a 12.2-mile stretch of abandoned railroad running between Gardiner and New Paltz. The rail trail continues further into Rosendale and ends at an old rail bridge over the Rondout Creek, but that section is not maintained by the association. The bridge you see from the Wallkill was fixed up in the early 1990s through a volunteer cooperative effort of New Paltz residents and the nearby Bruderhof community. Continue north about a mile and a quarter. On your right you will see a stream, which snakes through the woods as it meanders towards Cameo Lake on the other side of SR-32. Even when the water level is low, the stream is worth a short detour, for you might well surprise a flock of ducks or a solitary blue heron. From here, continue north a little less than a mile, and you will see the next boat launch on your left.

From the Springtown Road boat launch in Rosendale downstream, the Wallkill twists and turns as it gradually heads north and east. On your right, a windmill towers above the trees, standing out against the natural backdrop. You will parallel SR-213, going under SR-32, the New York State Thruway and, finally, the historic Perrine's Bridge, a covered bridge built in 1844 and restored a century and a half later. Here the river becomes impassable, with the dam near Dashville Road blocking your way. This stretch between the last access and the dam is 4.25 miles.

From the SR-213 access points, you can paddle north towards Sturgeon Pool where the Wallkill, for all intents and purposes, ends. Once again the river, for the most part, seems wild; then suddenly some man-made structure confronts you. It is precisely this juxtaposition of the natural and the manufactured that marks this river in Ulster County. Finally the vista opens up; you have reached Sturgeon Pool. You can swim in this pond; in fact, Central Hudson maintains a recreation area here for its employees. On the northern side of the pond, the Wallkill flows out and into the Rondout, but at this point it is not navigable. Depending on water levels, a kayak can continue into the Swartekill, a marshy area leading out of Sturgeon Pool on it northeast verge.

Helpful Web site:

http://www.dec.state.ny.us/website/dfwmr/fish/lakemaps/sturplmap.pdf offers a map of Sturgeon Pool. Though not meant for navigational use, the map gives water surface area, depths, contours, and species of fish found.

▶ **Wallkill River from New Paltz to Rifton**

Ulster County
Ponds and Lakes

U-10– U-15

U-10 Alder Lake in Hardenburgh

■ **How to get there:** From I-84 take exit 4W to SR-17 (future I-86) West. Stay on SR-17 for 41 miles, then exit in Livingston Manor (exit 96). Turn right onto Debruce Road (CR-81) heading west. Make your first right onto Old Route 17 (first CR-178, then CR-179). After 1.3 miles bear right at fork onto Beaver Kill Road (first CR-151, then CR-152) for 8 miles. As you leave Sullivan County, continue straight for 4 miles, though the name of the road changes to Turnwood Road (CR-54). In Turnwood, CR-54 turns sharply to the left and changes its name to Alder Lake Road. After about 2 miles, where Alder Lake Road ends and Cross Mountain Road begins, make a right turn into the park.

■ **Where to put in:** Access is difficult. The lake is a tenth of a mile from the parking lot, so you will need to carry your kayak to the launch area.

■ **Remarks:** The Department of Environmental Conservation maintains this remote and beautiful 44-acre lake in the 13,500-acre Balsam Lake Mountain Wild Forest. A mile and a half trail loops the lake, which is stocked with trout. There is no day-use charge to park, and a New York State boating permit is not required.

Web sites:

• http://www.dec.state.ny.us/website/dlf/publands/cats/balsam.html gives information including the history of, the activities supported by, and the access points in the Balsam Lake Mountain Wild Forest. Alder Lake is part of this forest.

• http://www.dec.state.ny.us/website/dfwmr/fish/lakemaps/aldrlkmap. pdf offers a map of Alder Lake. Though not meant for navigational use, the map gives water surface area, depths, contours, and species of fish found.

U-11 Lake Minnewaska in Gardiner
(Minnewaska State Park Preserve)

■ **How to get there:** Take the New York State Thruway (I-87) to exit 17, New Paltz. Turn left onto State Route 299 (SR-299). Go through the village of New Paltz and continue until SR-299 ends, a total of 7 miles. Turn right onto US-44/SR-55 West and follow it for 4.5 miles as it climbs the mountain, goes around the hairpin turn, and passes the Trapps, an area well known for technical climbing. The entrance to Minnewaska State Park is on your left.

■ **Where to put in:** After the gatehouse, follow the road as it winds and climbs towards the lake. Turn left past a maintenance building before you reach the parking areas. To the left of a bank of porta-potties is a lake-access area for boaters and divers. Unload your kayak here and carry it down a somewhat steeply graded gravel path to the lake. Once down, it is easy to launch into this sheltered cove.

■ **Remarks:** Surrounded by dramatic cliffs and dense forests, the 23-acre lake is crystal clear and beautiful. The park itself is often crowded, especially on summer weekends, but kayaking on the lake (which, incidentally, rents no boats) assures you quiet and seclusion. The park charges a daily entrance fee and honors the Empire Pass, an annual fee that covers admission to all New York State parks from April 1 to March 31. In addition you must have a Palisades Interstate Park Commission boating permit, which may be used at several other Mid-Hudson Valley lakes as well. You may purchase the permit at the park office at the Peterskill parking lot about a half a mile east on US-44/SR-55.

Web site:
• http://nysparks.state.ny.us/parks/info.asp?parkID=78
gives information about the use of the park.

U-12 Onteora Lake in Kingston

■ **How to get there:** From the New York State Thruway (I-87), take exit 19, Kingston. At the rotary after the toll booth, take State Route 28 (SR-28) West. Stay on SR-28 for 4 miles. After Waughkonk Road turn right onto an unmarked road, the entrance to the park.

▶ **Ulster County Ponds and Lakes**

■ **Where to put in:** From the parking lot walk down towards the lake.

■ **Remarks:** This 18.5-acre lake and the area surrounding it are amazingly rustic for their location within the city of Kingston bounds.

Web site:

• http://www.dec.state.ny.us/website/dfwmr/fish/lakemaps/ontelkmap. pdf offers a map of Onteora Lake. Though not meant for navigational use, the map gives water surface area, depths, contours, and species of fish found.

U-13 Tillson Lake in Gardiner

■ **How to get there:** From I-87 take exit 18 to New Paltz. Turn left onto State Route 299 (SR-299). Go through the village and continue 7 miles until SR-299 ends. Turn left onto US-44/SR-55 for one mile. Bear right onto North Mountain Road. Continue for 2 miles to a stop sign. Here the name changes to South Mountain Road. Continue straight for 1.5 miles. Turn right onto Beecher Hill Road. At one mile the road ends: to the right is Aumick Road; to the left is the unmarked Lake Road. Turn left. On your left you will see the lake and a parking area.

■ **Where to put in:** Access to the lake from the parking lot is easy.

■ **Remarks:** New York State acquired the 22-acre lake in the spring of 2006 as part of a settlement of a local environmental controversy. A coalition of local environmentalists fought a proposal for massive development of the Shawangunk ridge. The Tillson Lake area was slated for construction of a 296-acre golf course. Management of the site now falls under the purview of Minnewaska State Park. The area around the lake situated at the bottom of the ridge is wooded and largely undeveloped. New York State requires a boat permit, which can be purchased for an annual fee. At the time of this writing, there is no gatehouse and no admission charge.

U-14 Upper Pond in Woodstock
(Kenneth L. Wilson Campground)

■ **How to get there:** From the New York State Thruway, take exit 19, Kingston. At the rotary after the tollbooth, take State Route 28 (SR-28)

West. Look for the turnoff for Woodstock (SR-375); 1.4 miles after that intersection, turn right onto Old Route 28. Stay on it for half a mile, turning right onto Ohayo Mountain Road, also known as County Route 41 (CR-41). Go a few hundred feet and make a left onto CR-40 (Glenford Wittenberg Road). Continue on CR-40 for 6.6 miles. The campground is on your left.

■ **Where to put in:** The boat launch is all the way to the left of the large parking area provided for beach and day access.

■ **Remarks:** This DEC campground is open for day use. There are two small ponds here, Upper Pond and Lower Pond. Small boats with no engines are permitted on Upper Pond. Although the two ponds are contiguous, a dam prevents access to Lower Pond. Surrounded by the Catskills, the park offers truly impressive views. There is a nominal daily use fee; no boating permit is required.

Web site:

• http://www.dec.state.ny.us/website/do/camping/campgrounds/kenneth. html gives general information about the campground.

U-15 Yankeetown Pond in Woodstock

■ **How to get there:** From the New York State Thruway, take exit 19, Kingston. At the rotary after the toll booth, take State Route 28 (SR-28) West. Look for the turn-off for Woodstock (SR-375); 1.4 miles after that intersection, turn right onto Old Route 28. Stay on it for half a mile, turning right onto Ohayo Mountain Road, also known County Route 41 (CR-41). Go a few hundred feet and make a left onto CR-40 (Glenford Wittenberg Road). Continue on CR-40 for 3 miles. You will see the pond on your right. Turn right onto Pond Road. A pull-off on the right side of the road can accommodate quite a few cars.

■ **Where to put in:** The parking area is quite close to the edge of the pond. Boat access is relatively easy.

■ **Remarks:** The 44-acre pond is nestled in the Catskills and surrounded by low mountains and evergreen forests. The setting is idyllic, but be warned: in the summer the pond is overgrown with water lilies, and boating becomes impossible.

▶ **Ulster County Ponds and Lakes**

5

Columbia, Greene, and Other Nearby Counties

Back Bay

Give me the quiet water, give me the back bay,
Give me a good excuse to slip the strangle noose of a workday.
Oh, my soul is free, no one to bother me on the back bay.

> *Don't want your noisy engine, don't want the wind in my hair.*
> *Give me an old canoe, a paddle light and true—they will take me where*
> *The heron waits for the tide and fate to bring her dinner there.*

Give me the quiet water, give me the back bay,
I feel the need to ride the changes of the tide in the worst way.
Oh, I do believe I feel the river breathe on the back bay.

> *Oh you can keep the channel, you've got places to go.*
> *The river rushing by, you're living on the fly, I can take things slowly.*
> *I don't mind if I fall behind in the ebb and flow.*

We need that quiet water, we need the back bay,
A buffer from the storm, the place where life is born, where the cattails sway.
The river's health is in the secret wealth of the back bay.

Give me the quiet water: rock me in the cradle of the back bay.
We need that quiet water: share it with the eagle and the osprey.
Cherish the quiet water of the back bay.

Jean Valla McAvoy © 2000

Columbia County

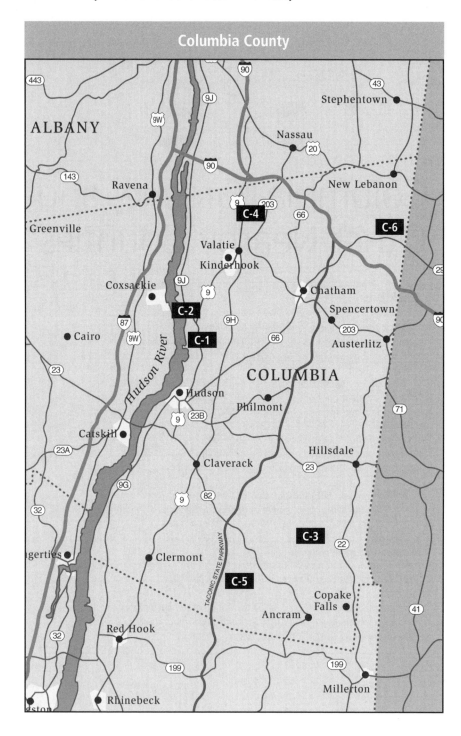

ALBANY

COLUMBIA

Hudson River

TACONIC STATE PARKWAY

Stephentown

Nassau

New Lebanon

Ravena

Greenville

Valatie

Kinderhook

Coxsackie

Chatham

Spencertown

Cairo

Austerlitz

Hudson

Philmont

Catskill

Hillsdale

Claverack

Clermont

Copake Falls

Ancram

Red Hook

Millerton

Rhinebeck

C-1   C-2   C-3   C-4   C-5   C-6

Stockport Creek to Claverack and Kinderhook Creeks
—*Eagles and Egrets, Beaches and Mudflats*
C-1

■ **Route:** From the launch, go east into Stockport Creek, later turning northeast into the confluence of the Claverack and Kinderhook creeks. Continue until the Kinderhook becomes impassable. Return to the mouth of Stockport Creek. Before leaving, take a short excursion to the southern tip of Stockport Middle Ground and back.

■ **Total Mileage:** 5+ miles.

■ **Difficulty:** Challenging. **R P C CH** (See page 18.)

■ **Setting:** Stockport Creek is a wide tributary with some marsh, some houses, docks, no-wake zone changing into woodlands as you go inland. Kinderhook and Claverack creeks are much narrower creeks than the Stockport, with forests on both sides, occasional houses where the creek approaches roads. The Hudson River section is very scenic with a sandy beach on the southern tip of the island of Stockport Middle Ground.

■ **Hazards:** Currents, tides, weather conditions, and boat traffic on the Hudson always pose some danger to small craft.

■ **Remarks:** The Claverack and Kinderhook creeks have some shallows and riffles that require some portaging depending on the season. Heavy rainfalls may make the riffles more difficult to portage. As you progress northward, the current and elevation changes eventually make it impossible to paddle. Do not stop at Stockport Middle Ground during nesting season—fortunately not the warm months most conducive to water activities. The island is a breeding area for bald eagles. During high tide the beach is under water.

This Stockport Creek run is a pleasure to kayak for its diverse ecology and biology. On a short trip, you paddle down a major tributary of the Hudson into a much narrower creek. You pass through freshwater tidal marshes into forest. Finally you cross a wide river alive with shipping and tides, and visit a sandy beach. You can see great egrets and eagles, watch muskrats and groundhogs, find wild rice and cattails, maple and oak.

Columbia County

C-1 Stockport Creek to Claverack and Kinderhook Creeks

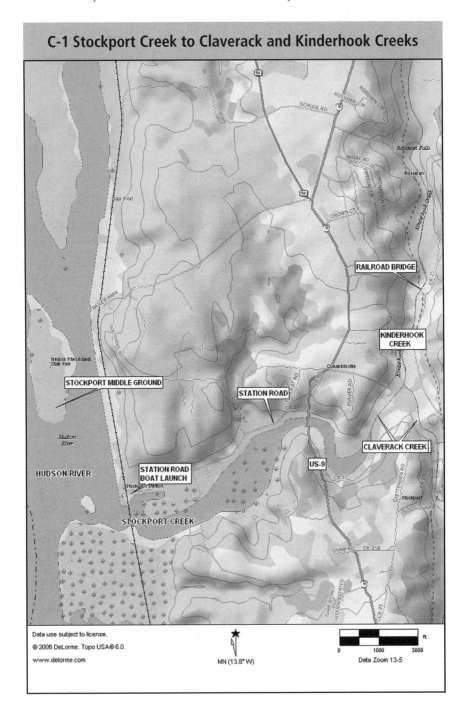

▶ **Stockport Creek to Claverack and Kinderhook Creeks**

Directions:

Take the New York State Thruway (I-87) to exit 21. Make an immediate left onto State Route 23B (SR-23B), and then another left onto SR-23 East over the Rip Van Winkle Bridge to the intersection with SR-9G. Turn left onto SR-9G North and follow it for 3.3 miles into the city of Hudson. Make a left onto US-9 North. Continue 5.5 miles into Stockport. (Or, from the southbound Taconic State Parkway, turn left onto SR-82, heading west-northwest for 5 miles. Take US-9 North—it will make some turns as it traverses the city of Hudson—about 11 miles into Stockport.) Turn left onto Station Road immediately after you go over Stockport Creek. The road ends at the Hudson River. Parking and a gravel boat ramp are on your left.

The Paddle:

Launch from the parking area right next to the Amtrak railroad into the mouth of Stockport Creek. Turn left and east, away from the railroad bridge. Stockport Creek here is wide, supporting motor craft as well as small boats. However, there is little boat traffic, and no-wake zone signs are clearly posted. On the northern side of the creek, you paddle by houses with docks, boats anchored to them. The opposite shore is more

As they approach the Hudson, the Claverack and Kinderhook converge forming the wide, much deeper Stockport Creek.

Columbia County

Facing south during low tide with a kayak beached
at the southern tip of Stockport Middle Ground.

deserted. As you continue eastward, the freshwater marshes on both sides give way to woods.

At about a mile, you approach the US-9 overpass. Here the creek gets shallower and rocky and, depending on rainfall and water levels, you may have to portage to go on. The creek continues fairly wide, twisting and turning, before it narrows considerably and heads north-northeast as the Claverack Creek. A quarter of a mile upstream, the Claverack turns sharply southward while you bear left, continuing on the Kinderhook. An old railroad bridge crosses the creek about a mile and a quarter farther. There are more riffles before, and again shortly after, the overpass. I pulled my kayak through each of the three rocky sections—it was a hot day and the cool water on my ankles was refreshing—but I turned around, exhausted, and went back when a quarter of a mile further I hit another longer and rockier stretch.

Before packing up to head home, take a quick look at the Stockport Flats area. Go under the Amtrak bridge into the Hudson. The island to your right is Stockport Middle Ground. Except during high tide, the southern tip is a sandy beach. Paddle the half mile there for a rest and some beautiful views.

▶ Stockport Creek to Claverack and Kinderhook Creeks

Stockport Flats Area
—Mudflats and Marshes

C-2

■ **Route:** From launch, enter the Hudson River heading north—passing to the right of Stockport Middle Ground, then to the left of Gay's Point—to the Ferry Road boat launch in Newton Hook. Return making a side trip into the inlet east of Gay's Point and then down the west side of Stockport Middle Ground.

■ **Total Mileage:** 9 miles—may easily be adjusted, shortened or lengthened.

■ **Difficulty:** Moderate. **CH C** (See page 18.)

■ **Setting:** Open river, inlets, marshes, hardwood forests.

■ **Hazards:** Currents, tides, weather conditions, and boat traffic on the Hudson always pose some danger to small craft.

■ **Remarks:** Do not stop at Stockport Middle Ground during nesting season—the island is a breeding area for bald eagles.

Today, when we think about dredging a river, we generally think about cleaning up hazardous wastes that communities and companies alike dumped into the waterways, never thinking about the eventual outcome, never wondering *what will happen to this raw sewage, these PCBs.* In the nineteenth and early twentieth centuries, however, rivers were dredged as part of a massive expansion of the transportation system, and communities near the rivers, as well as giant companies, were the beneficiaries of the ensuing economic boom. After the invention of the steamship, the Hudson River was dredged to accommodate the flourishing shipping industry, which needed deeper channels for the larger vessels. The material that was removed from the channels was deposited along the banks of the northern portions of the river. The dredging created mudflats north of the city of Hudson in Columbia County. One of these mudflats is now known now as Stockport Middle Ground. Many boats ran aground on Stockport Middle Ground because it was visible only during low tide. As a result the federal government funded the construction of the Hudson-Athens Lighthouse in 1874. With subsequent dredging and deposits of silt, this flat and Gay's Point, less than a mile north, became true land masses, no longer submerged by high tides. The inadvertent result of these changes to the natural

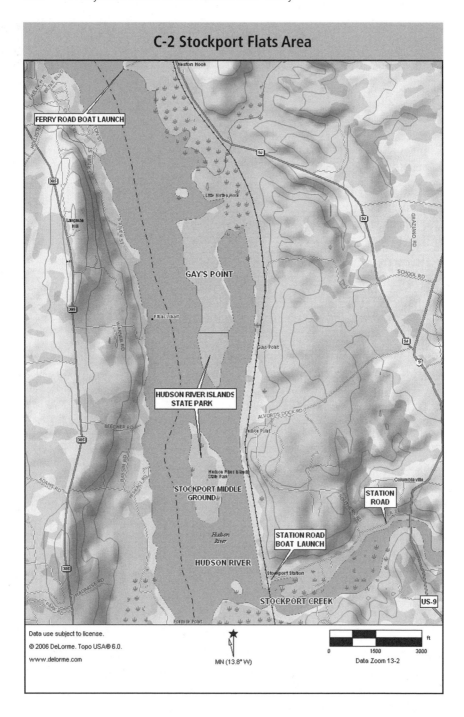

C-2 Stockport Flats Area

▶ **Stockport Flats Area**

environment is the Stockport Flats, today a marsh area providing habitat to a variety of plant, fish, mammalian and bird life.

Directions:
Take the New York State Thruway (I-87) to exit 21. Make an immediate left onto State Route 23B (SR-23B) and then another left onto SR-23 East over the Rip Van Winkle Bridge to the intersection with SR-9G. Turn left onto SR-9G North and follow it for 3.3 miles into the city of Hudson. Make a left onto US-9 North. Continue 5.5 miles into Stockport. (Or, from the southern Taconic State Parkway, turn left onto SR-82, heading west-north-west for 5 miles. Take US-9 North—it will make some turns as it traverses the city of Hudson—about 11 miles into Stockport.) Turn left onto Station Road immediately after you go over the Stockport Creek. The road ends at the Hudson River. Parking and a gravel boat ramp are on your left.

The Paddle:
The launch is the same for the creek and for the flats. To explore the flats, turn right and go under the bridge into the Hudson River. The view here is impressive—water everywhere. Behind you is the wide mouth of Stockport Creek. Look downriver towards Hudson and Athens: the silhouettes of low mountains rise in the distance. Look north: the river divides as it flows around the island of Stockport Middle Ground, the peninsula of Gay's Point, and beyond that, Coxsackie Island.

Turn northward, passing to the right of Stockport Middle Ground, avoiding the choppier water churned up by the boats traveling in the deep shipping channel west of the island. During summer months water chestnuts grow between the island and the shore. During high tide you can pass on either side of these dense clusters, but as the tide recedes, the east bank of the island becomes less accessible.

Continue northward around the peninsula, keeping Gay's Point to your right. Stockport Middle Ground and the southern portion of Gay's Point comprise the Hudson River Islands State Park, accessible only by water. Picnic tables and rustic campsites with sandy beaches dot the west shore of the peninsula. The landscape changes as you pass the park boundary. Now the trees come closer to the river's edge. Look for bald eagles perched high in the branches.

Columbia County

As I paddled by recently, an adult eagle with the characteristic white head soared, circled and dove. Juveniles, with their darker plumage, flew from the trees, most likely flushed out by my kayak. An Audubon naturalist had warned me that kayaks and canoes pose a greater danger for the eagles than motorized craft. The eagles hear motorboats well in advance of their appearance. The unexpected appearance of quiet kayaks and canoes apparently scare them, however—and suddenly surprised nesting birds have been known to abandon their nests.

Above Gay's Point you should explore several plant-filled marshes where native cattails, pickerelweed, and spatterdock vie for sustenance with the invasive water chestnut. Duck under one of the railroad trestles and most likely you will find a small inlet on the other side choked with water chestnuts. In the Nutten Hook area about a mile above Gay's Point, the Ferry Road river access and boat launch juts into the Hudson. Just north of this, the topography of the shore changes, with rocky outcroppings descending dramatically to the river. You can explore further—there are some additional marshes less than half a mile north of here—or turn back.

Facing Stockport Middle Ground and Gay's Point, paddle northward into the Hudson.

▶ **Stockport Flats Area**

Hudson River Islands State Park, Gay's Point Section, straddles the southern half of the peninsula of Gay's Point and the island, Stockport Middle Ground. Here find picnic tables, beaches, and camping sites.

On your return trip take a detour into the finger of water between the east side of Gay's Point and the shore. Many birds favor the marshes, and you may see some plovers or catch sight of a green heron. The water chestnut here is dense, clogging most of the inlet. Stay towards the eastern side. There, a slightly deeper channel remains free of vegetation.

If water conditions are favorable, swing into the main portion of the Hudson, passing Stockport Middle Ground—also part of the Hudson River Islands State Park—on its other side. A sandy beach spans the entire western coast of the island. Here you can pull over for a picnic and a rest. As you head the short way back to the Stockport boat access, notice the height of the sand piled up towards the base of the island—an imposing twenty-five-foot high hill of sand, all dredged from the river bottom.

Helpful Web site:
• http://nerrs.noaa.gov/HudsonRiver/StockportFlats.html
offers limited information about the geology, the biology, and the history of the area.

Columbia County

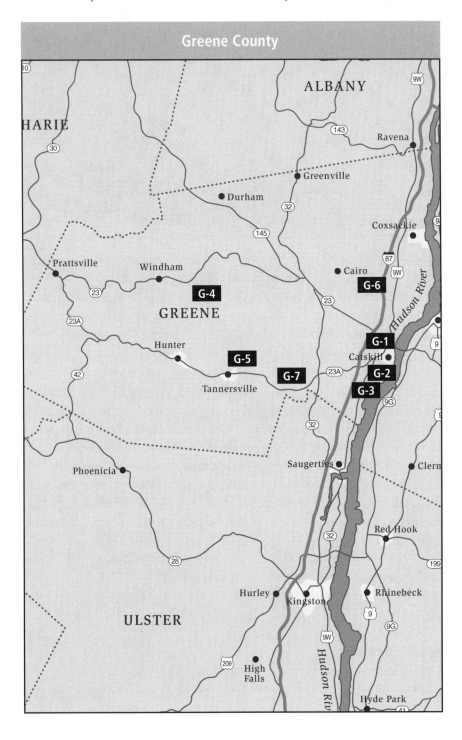

Greene County

Catskill Creek in Catskill
—Boats, Bridges, and Solitude

G-1

After nearly forty miles crossing and descending through Schoharie, Albany, and Greene counties, Catskill Creek joins the Hudson River in the village of Catskill. Catskill Point stands at this crossroads, a curious mix of the cultural and economic history of the region. Prior to European settlement and colonization, the creek served as a natural divide between two indigenous tribes, the Esopus and Mahican. In its early history, the village of Catskill flourished and became known for its grain market and flour mills situated near a falls on the creek. Following the War of 1812, the tanning industry grew, using the tannin of the hemlock forests of Greene County to process and preserve hides. In an early warning against unbridled greed and a shortsighted disregard for both the economy and the environment, the hemlock forests were eventually depleted. The tanning industry abandoned the area, simply picking up and moving west. Fortunately, the invention of the steamboat allowed tourism, art, and new industries, most notably the harvesting of ice for distribution in New York City, to salvage what might well have been a dying region. Thomas Cole settled in Catskill and immortalized the beauty of this part of New York with his famous landscapes. Here Frederic Church studied under Cole and then settled across the river at Olana. With the settling in Catskill and Hudson of these two artists, the Hudson River School of painting emerged, helping to popularize the area. Facilitated by easy access by boat, the Catskill Mountains became a preeminent resort area, with Catskill Point as the landing where tourists from the city disembarked and headed inland.

Later technological advances in transportation would again irrevocably change the area. As the automobile replaced the steamboat, roads replaced rivers. The Hudson no longer served as the main transportation route north, and Catskill was no longer a waypoint en route to the mountains. But to this day, the village retains some vestiges of its history.

■ **Route:** After launching from Dutchman's Landing, paddle around Catskill Point into the mouth of the creek. Follow the creek, passing under the US-9W overpass. At the old dam, turn around and return.
■ **Total Mileage:** 5.4 miles round trip.

■ **Difficulty:** Moderate. **CH C** (See page 18.)

■ **Setting:** Hudson River into the wide channel of the mouth of the Catskill. Pass first through old industrial Catskill, then through residential section, and finally out of town and into woods.

■ **Hazards:** Currents, tides, weather conditions, and boat traffic on the Hudson always pose some danger to small craft.

■ **Remarks:** Short trip offers great variety of scenery.

Directions to Dutchman's Landing:

Get off the NYS Thruway at exit 21 and follow the signs into Catskill, getting onto State Route 23B (SR-23B), which becomes Main Street in the village. Stay on Main Street for about 2.5 miles. You will see Catskill Creek on your right. Shortly before the road ends, turn left into Dutchman's Landing, which is clearly labeled and offers plenty of parking and easy access to the Hudson.

Directions to the alternative West Main Street boat launch:

From SR-23B, turn right onto Bridge Street and cross over the creek. Make first right onto West Main Street. Parking is on your right to the right of the high-school parking lot. This alternative launch allows you to explore Catskill Creek without paddling in the Hudson River. Thus, this can be regarded as an easy paddle.

The Paddle:

Launch your kayak in the Hudson River and head south around Catskill Point into the mouth of Catskill Creek. The creek here is several hundred feet wide and, depending on weather and boat traffic, may be choppy. Clear indicators of the importance of industry and transportation, large gasoline tanks and marinas border the banks. As you paddle further, the creek narrows somewhat and the commercial buildings give way to residential ones—though these are not the huge new waterfront houses of many more affluent towns.

One mile from the entrance to the creek, you will go under the first of four overpasses. Bridge Street (SR-385) traverses the Uncle Sam Bridge, built in 1930 as a drawbridge and renovated 60 years later. A tenth of a mile further, on your left, you can see the West Main Street boat launch and the campus of Catskill High School. The banks of the creek are now

▶ Catskill Creek in Catskill

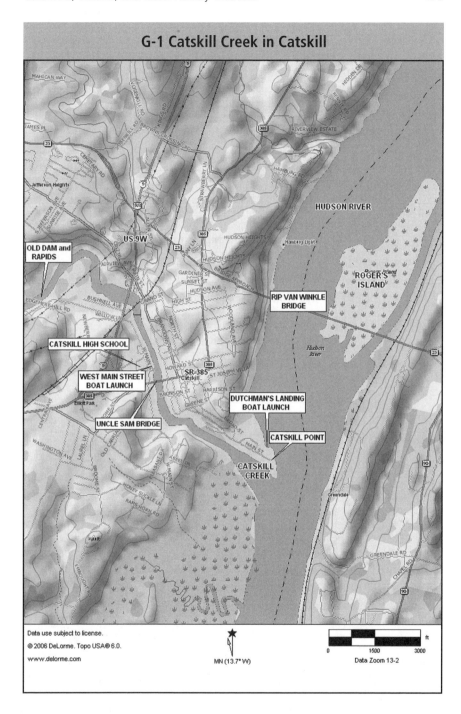

G-1 Catskill Creek in Catskill

HUDSON RIVER

US 9W

OLD DAM and RAPIDS

ROGER'S ISLAND

RIP VAN WINKLE BRIDGE

CATSKILL HIGH SCHOOL

Hudson River

WEST MAIN STREET BOAT LAUNCH

SR-385 Catskill

DUTCHMAN'S LANDING BOAT LAUNCH

UNCLE SAM BRIDGE

CATSKILL POINT

CATSKILL CREEK

Greendale

Data use subject to license.

© 2006 DeLorme. Topo USA® 6.0.

www.delorme.com

MN (13.7° W)

ft

0   1500   3000

Data Zoom 13-2

Greene County

less populated. Continue upstream another third of a mile and you see ahead, in close succession, three bridges crossing the creek. The first is now used only by pedestrians. The next is a railroad bridge used by CSXT freight trains, and the last is the US-9W overpass. Pass beneath the bridges and the scenery changes radically. You have left the congestion of the village with its numerous signs of commerce. There are not many houses here. Gone is the deep channel of water that allows motorized craft access to the Hudson. Now you can see the creek bottom, with rock ledges and slabs. The adjacent roads recede and the sides of the creek rise, sometimes dramatically, the woods offering a haven to wildlife.

Armed with my Hudson Valley maps and my enthusiasm, I set out on this trip hoping to reach the confluence of the Kaaterskill and Catskill creeks. I knew it was not far. Unfortunately, after paddling under the power line and rounding a bend and heading southwest, I heard the telltale sound of gushing water. I saw stanchions standing useless in the

A succession of overpasses on the Catskill separates the urban from the rural landscapes.

▶ Catskill Creek in Catskill

An old dam, rocks, and rapids prevent further exploration of the Catskill Creek.

water, vestiges of some earlier time and some abandoned road. A little further ahead on the right bank stood a dilapidated building, a mill perhaps. Crossing the creek is an old dam, one side totally collapsed, the other still holding, and a current too strong to paddle against. Disappointed, I vowed I would try again. But next time I would go prepared to portage, when the weather was warmer and when getting wet would be invigorating rather than a hardship.

If you return to Dutchman's Landing and want to paddle further, consider a trip around Roger's Island. Lying beneath the Rip Van Winkle Bridge, the pretty island, owned by the DEC, offers marshland to explore and a beach on the west side where you can stop when the tide is not high.

Greene County

G-2 Dubois Creek into the RamsHorn-Livingston Sanctuary
—Diverse Terrain

- **Route:** From Dutchman's Landing in Catskill, head south, then immediately after rounding Catskill Point, turn west into the Catskill Creek; enter Dubois Creek and continue until you can go no farther.
- **Total Mileage:** 2.6 miles—subject to change depending on conditions.
- **Difficulty:** Moderate. **CH C** (See page 18.)
- **Setting:** Mixed woods, marsh, some fields.
- **Hazards:** Currents, tides, weather conditions, and boat traffic on the Hudson always pose some danger to small craft.
- **Remarks:** Area is best explored during mid to high tides.

The Hudson River is rich with history. Before Europeans colonized this part of the world or even explored it, Native Americans put their small boats into the Hudson, and those few sites that have now been protected through the foresight of conservationists provide venues to experience what those native people must have experienced three, four, five centuries ago. By the nineteenth century, the descendants of the colonists had put the river to work for them, providing a transportation system and a power system that fueled industrialization. Today, life on the Hudson reflects the economic changes nationwide from a manufacturing to a service economy. While many of the towns have renovated their waterfronts, replacing factories with art galleries and warehouses with antique stores, some town and cities, like Catskill, retain these vestiges of the past, a reminder of their history.

Directions:
Take exit 21 off the NYS Thruway and follow the signs into Catskill, getting onto State Route 23B (SR-23B), which becomes Main Street in the village. Stay on Main Street for about 2.5 miles. You will see Catskill Creek on your right. Shortly before the road ends, turn left into Dutchman's Landing, which is clearly labeled and offers plenty of parking, and ample and easy access to the Hudson.

▶ Dubois Creek into the RamsHorn-Livingston Sanctuary

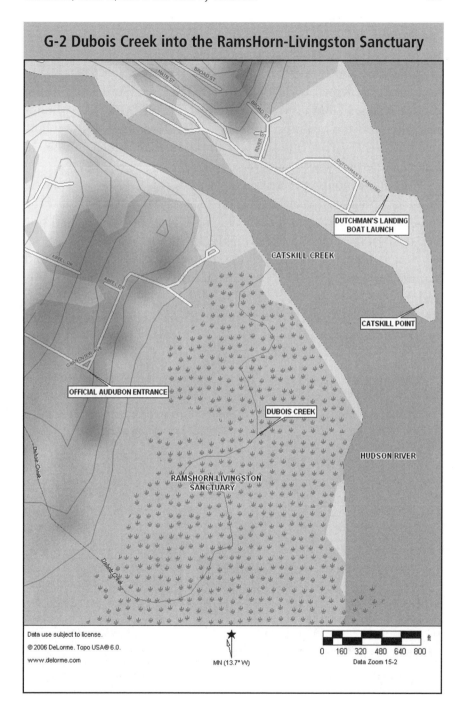

G-2 Dubois Creek into the RamsHorn-Livingston Sanctuary

DUTCHMAN'S LANDING BOAT LAUNCH

CATSKILL CREEK

CATSKILL POINT

OFFICIAL AUDUBON ENTRANCE

DUBOIS CREEK

HUDSON RIVER

RAMSHORN-LIVINGSTON SANCTUARY

Data use subject to license.

© 2006 DeLorme. Topo USA® 6.0.

www.delorme.com

MN (13.7° W)

0   160   320   480   640   800   ft

Data Zoom 15-2

The Paddle:

Put in your boat at Dutchman's Landing, heading south. Go around Catskill Point and turn right into the mouth of Catskill Creek. Look around. The park and marina may well be the town's future. But notice also the huge oil tanks on your right and all the old brick factory buildings. They provide a glimpse of what the Hudson was—of the industrialization the river facilitated, and the industrialization that almost destroyed the river itself.

Here at the mouth, the creek is very wide. Cross the creek and paddle on the far shore, staying away from the larger boats that tend to use the middle of the waterway. A quarter of a mile from the point as the crow flies, the mouth of Dubois Creek opens up. Turn left into it.

Not so long ago, this part of the reserve was clearly private. Ahead is a run-down building, along with what looks like an abandoned VW, rowboat, and power boat. Look behind you and there, standing tall, ominous, and industrial, are several Exxon tanks. As I explored this creek for the first time, I had just left the magic of RamsHorn Creek and I was at

Trees along the edge of Dubois Creek bear clear evidence of the presence of beaver.

▶ Dubois Creek into the RamsHorn-Livingston Sanctuary

A juvenile eagle perches on a snag in the RamsHorn-Livingston Sanctuary.

first sorely disappointed. But that was only until I rounded a bend and saw, perched in a tree not a hundred yards ahead, an osprey. My paddling disturbed him and he flew. When I went around another turn, a beaver swam right in front of my kayak towards the water's edge and then surface-dove into a lodge. Though the ecology of the sanctuary seems less unusual from the vantage point of Dubois Creek than it does from the RamsHorn, it is also more diverse. Round a bend and there is a marsh— no overhanging trees, just grasses and cattails. Round another and there is a meadow, perhaps formerly a field that was farmed. Turn once more and you are in a forest. Here, too, there is a maze of side channels, which you can attempt to paddle. But ultimately you can go no further, even down the main course. So you head back. If you still have energy, time, and desire, you can explore the Catskill Creek or spend some time paddling on the Hudson.

Helpful Web site:
• http://ny.audubon.org/RamsHorn.htm
  offers some basic information about the sanctuary and programs offered.

Greene County

G-3   RamsHorn Creek into the RamsHorn-Livingston Sanctuary
—Teeming with Wildlife

- **Route:** From Dutchman's Landing in Catskill, go south to the mouth of the RamsHorn; follow the creek as far as possible, then return to the launch site.
- **Total Mileage:** About 4.5 miles round trip.
- **Difficulty:** Moderate. **CH C** (See page 18.)
- **Setting:** Mixed woods edged by wetland vegetation.
- **Hazards:** Currents, tides, weather conditions, and boat traffic on the Hudson always pose some danger to small craft.
- **Remarks:** The creek is best explored during mid to high tides.

Just south of Catskill Creek on the west bank of the Hudson River lie between four and five hundred acres of forever-wild marsh and woodlands, cooperatively owned and managed by the Scenic Hudson Land Trust and the National Audubon Society. The sanctuary serves as a feeding and nesting area for both waterfowl and migratory birds, and its waters serve as an important breeding ground for bass and shad. The official Web sites of the sponsoring organizations describe the 480-acre reserve as the largest tidal swamp forest on the Hudson, and that description captures the place's unusual terrain. It is indeed tidal, and that means the water levels vary with the tides. Before heading out on a day trip, you want to check a tide chart and plan to go as close to high tide as possible. High tide is different on different spots on the Hudson; it is later the farther north you go, so check a chart for Catskill or a nearby town. The term "swamp forest" likewise catches the peculiar ecology of the spot. My first time touring the sanctuary, I was expecting to find a wetland similar to Tivoli Bay or Constitution Marsh, but I was surprised by the uniqueness and the enchantment of the spot.

The Audubon Society has its own canoe and kayak launch accessible from its parking lot on Dubois Road. To get to it, however, entails a half-mile walk from the parking lot. So, most likely, you will want to put in at Dutchman's Landing, a public park situated right on Catskill Point, which juts into the Hudson River right above the mouth of the Catskill Creek.

▶ **RamsHorn Creek into the RamsHorn-Livingston Sanctuary**

G-3 RamsHorn Creek into the RamsHorn-Livingston Sanctuary

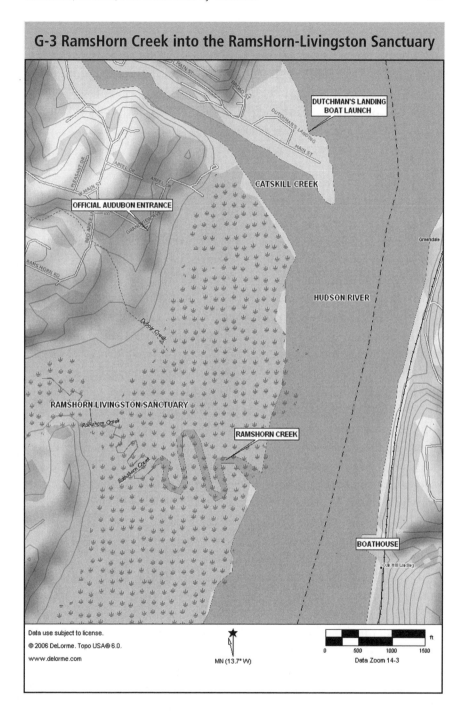

Directions:
Get off the NYS Thruway at exit 21 and follow the signs into Catskill, getting onto State Route 23B (SR-23B), which becomes Main Street in the village. Stay on Main Street for about 2.5 miles. You will see Catskill Creek on your right. Shortly before the road ends, turn left into Dutchman's Landing, which is clearly labeled and offers plenty of parking, and ample and easy access to the Hudson.

The Paddle:
Put in at Dutchman's Landing and head south, crossing the mouth of Catskill Creek. On your right is the RamsHorn-Livingston Sanctuary. If you stay near the shore, you will see a channel or two that wind their way into the preserve. You can paddle down these, but in a little while they will dead-end. The mouth of RamsHorn Creek is one mile south of where you put in. It is not as big as Catskill Creek, but clearly larger than the small channels. For a landmark, look at the opposite shore of the Hudson for a small, white, one-story boathouse standing alone. This used to belong to the Livingstons, the same family that turned over much of the reserve land to the stewardship of environmental groups. Turn in. Suddenly, a distinctive landscape unfolds. Here the forest comes close to the water's edge, but the final foot or two of shoreline is covered with a copious growth of very green wetland vegetation. As you venture in, first the quiet, then the sounds of birds calling and insects chittering replace the sounds of civilization—until you are brought back to the reality of place and time with the Amtrak train horn resounding from the other side of the river. As you go further down the creek, several bends make it difficult to distinguish between the main channel and the lesser side channels. Try some of the side channels. Eventually they become shallow and blocked by fallen logs and branches.

I paddled the creek on my own, enjoying it thoroughly, but decided to return for an interpretive kayak tour. Larry Federman, a naturalist, educator, and assistant warden of the sanctuary, led me through the winding creek, explaining some of its history—the twists and turns man-made by hunters to create backwater environments attractive to ducks—and pointing out some of the birds—the blue-gray gnatcatcher, tiny and shy, a flicker feeding its babies, a juvenile eagle identifiable by its dark plumage. We made our way leisurely to the Hudson, eventually veering

RamsHorn Creek into the RamsHorn-Livingston Sanctuary

Our kayaks startle a newborn fawn hiding in the tall grasses by the edge of the creek.

left into the marsh, where we turned around. As we headed back to the dock, we startled a large doe. She snorted, turned, and took off through the woods. A moment later her fawn stood up, half hidden by the tall grasses, and teetered, wanting to follow, but too young to walk.

I paddled back thankful for a wilderness adventure rarely experienced today.

Helpful Web site:
• http://ny.audubon.org/RamsHorn.htm offers some basic information about the sanctuary and programs offered.

Sullivan, Sussex, Rockland, and Westchester Counties

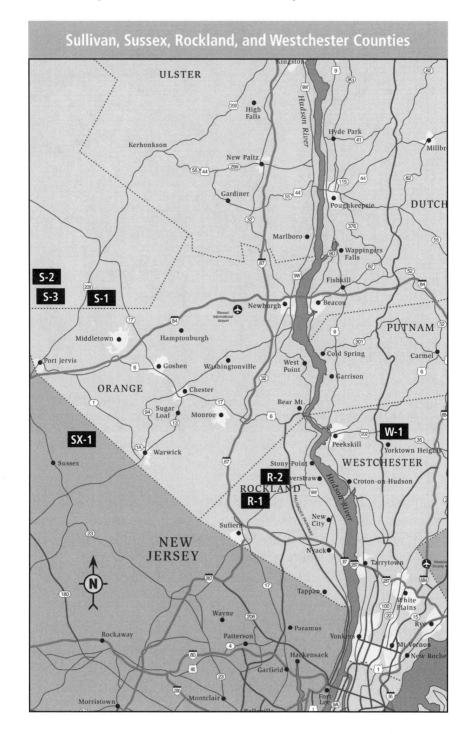

The Bashakill
—Wilderness Beckons

S-1

■ **Route:** From the northernmost DEC boat launch on the west side of the Bashakill, going south-southwest through the Bashakill.

■ **Total Mileage:** Up to 8 miles round trip.

■ **Difficulty:** Easy.

■ **Setting:** Large, protected wetland area between the Shawangunk Mountains on the east and the Allegheny Plateau (with the Poconos towards the south and the Catskills towards the north), comprised of marsh and open water, woods, fields, and abandoned orchards.

■ **Hazards:** None.

■ **Remarks:** Seasonally dense aquatic vegetation, including a profusion of water lilies, may prove difficult to paddle through.

I'd asked an acquaintance of mine, an avid canoeist and fisherman who'd grown up in Orange County, to recommend a local place for me to kayak. He considered only a few moments and then suggested the Bashakill Swamp. I'd never heard of it, but I was immediately intrigued since my first kayaking experiences in marshes and bogs had revealed a covert setting with a wealth of wildlife. Though he'd provided the name, he'd neglected to give me directions or specific information about the swamp. My preliminary research was fraught with difficulty for several reasons. There seems to be no definitive spelling of Bashakill, which is alternatively written as Bashakill, Basherkill, Basha Kill, and Basher Kill. Look up Basher Kill on the Internet and you will uncover Web site upon Web site devoted to the violence suggested by the words. Furthermore, while locals refer to the Bashakill *Swamp* or simply to the Bashakill, most maps label it, instead, Bashakill Lake.

To accommodate the many outdoors people the spot attracts—birders, fishermen, hikers, kayakers—the DEC has set aside several areas for parking. Not all have easy access for small boats, but the three shown on the map do. Incidentally, only electric motors are permitted on the lake, thus limiting noise and preventing gasoline pollution. Haven Road offers a fourth possibility for launching a kayak. You can put into the water at the bridge, and then move your car to the lot west of the Bashakill.

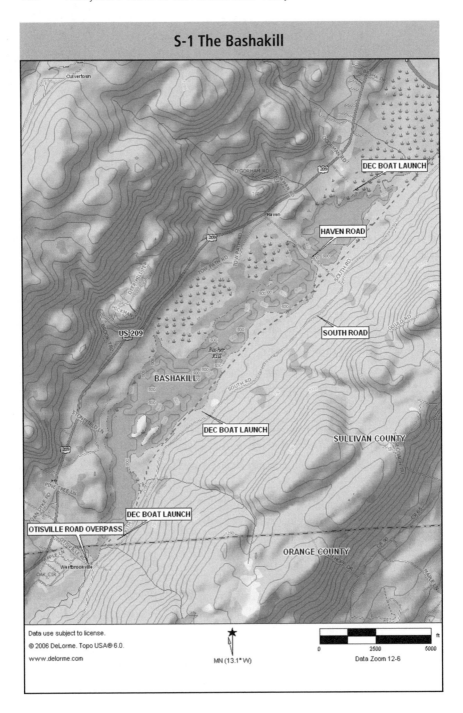

▶ The Bashakill

Directions to the northernmost of the boat launches:
Take State Route 17 (SR-17) West (or the future I-86) into Wurtsboro (exit 113). Turn onto US-209 South. Continue 1.2 miles. On your left you will see a DEC sign for the access.

Directions to the second of the boat launches:
Continue south on US-209 another .7 mile and make a left onto Haven Road. On the other side of the Bashakill, turn right onto South Road. Stay on South Road for 1.7 miles. The parking area is clearly marked on your right.

Directions to the southernmost of the boat launches:
Should you decide to start your trip from the southern end of the Bashakill, go a total of 2.8 miles after your left turn from Haven Road onto South Road. There you will find a small parking area from which you can begin your paddle northwards.

The Paddle:
As you approach the water from the northernmost launch, the stream lies to your left and an impressive vista of the wetlands opens up to your right. The water is clear and the fish easily visible, especially so after the vegetation dies back in late fall and before it takes off in the spring. Head south. In summer you must find your way through open channels through the plants, which brush the bottom of your boat, impeding your progress. In less than a mile go under Haven Road, a one-lane bridge, a favorite spot for fishermen. Now the landscape opens up further with wide views of the ridges, east and west. As you continue, look for a stand of dead pines on the west side, a favorite nesting place for ospreys. A little more than a mile and half from Haven Road, you will see a narrow waterway entering from the left. That is the next boat launch.

Paddle slowly and watch carefully and you will see a multitude of bird life. Bald eagles nest in the area of the two islands. If you do not spot an eagle, you may see an eagle nest later in the season after the foliage drops. Large numbers of Canada geese and the much more unusual wood ducks gather here in the fall. If you have never seen wood ducks, their harlequin markings are striking, as is their habit, unusual for a duck, of perching in trees. The west side of the island, more isolated, offers excellent opportunities for observing wildlife, but in late summer the dense growth of water plants blocks access to the far side. Continue south. The Bashakill, still wide, meanders back and forth another two miles or so, gradually making its way to the southernmost boat launch. Go a bit further south, stopping just before Otisville Road. There the water narrows dramatically, the current picks up, and the elevation drops. The swamp is funneled into the fast-moving creek that will feed into the Neversink as it makes its way towards the Delaware River.

A bit of local history—the old Delaware and Hudson Canal, a nineteenth-century engineering feat, allowed Pennsylvania's anthracite coal to be shipped via barges pulled by mules, first along the Delaware, then through New York State to the Rondout, and finally up the Hudson River to Canada and down the river to New York City. The towpath parallels the west side of the Wildlife Area. Its replacement, the D&H Railway, ran along the east bank where it now serves as a hiking trail.

Before wetlands were protected, the area was drained annually and farmed. With a renewed awareness of the importance of protecting our

Shortly before it empties into the Neversink on its way to the Delaware, the Bashakill opens into several miles of wetland and swamp

▶ **The Bashakill**

An eagle perched in a tree watches over the Bashakill wetland and swamp.

natural resources, New York State set up the Department of Environmental Conservation in 1970, and two years later the state acquired the largest wetland area of southeastern New York. This acquisition was the Basha Kill Wildlife Management Area, over 2,200 acres of wetlands protected and overseen by the DEC and boasting over thirty species of fish and over 200 species of birds.

Helpful Web sites:
- http://www.thebashakill.org/wildlife.htm
  offers information on the birds and the habitat.

- http://www.catskillhikes.com/
  gives basic information on the wetlands and the wildlife as well as the Basha Kill Area Association, a group that works to preserve the area.

- http://www.shawangunkridge.org/bkevents.htm
  lists free guided field trips to the area.

Sullivan County

SX-1 The Wallkill River National Wildlife Refuge
—Pristine and Protected

- **Route:** Three parking areas allow for following the river either north-wards or southwards; the route here launches from the County Route 565 (CR-565) access and proceeds northward through the refuge.
- **Total Mileage:** About 11 miles of paddling within the preserve, one way; additional possible mileage to the north and south of preserve.
- **Difficulty:** Moderate. **R P D** (See page 18.)
- **Setting:** Marsh, grassland, shrubland, wetland forests, upland forests.
- **Hazards:** Some very short and easy rapids; occasional deadfall; a very low footbridge.
- **Remarks:** You will very likely have to portage, but portages here are easy. In midsummer and in drought conditions, the river is extremely shallow and may be impassable. Conversely, after heavy rains or snow-melt the current may be strong enough to make paddling southward—against the current—difficult.

Everyone knows about our national parks with their famed geysers and hot springs, mountain peaks and canyons, bears and eagles, but fewer people by far are aware of the more extensive National Wildlife Refuge System, which protects the wildlife and habitat in 540 separate refuges around our country. Just crossing the border into Orange County in New York and lying mainly in Sussex County, New Jersey, but near the Mid-Hudson Valley, the Wallkill River National Wildlife Refuge is an impres-sive sanctuary easily accessible by small boat.

With the arrival of Europeans in New York State, a number of villages sprang up all along the Wallkill River, taking advantage of the benefits of a riverside location for transportation and power. In between these villages lie stretches of farmland. These tracts of land also benefited from the river, using its water for irrigation and enjoy-ing the fertility of land enriched by frequent flooding. These two, disparate uses of the river historically have caused conflict, but as you head towards Lake Mohawk, where the Wallkill originates, and as you cross the state line into New Jersey and enter the refuge, sud-denly the setting becomes more desolate, more wild. Absent here are the dams, the factories, the farmhouses and the silos. The river here

▶ **The Wallkill River National Wildlife Refuge**

SX-1 The Wallkill River National Wildlife Refuge

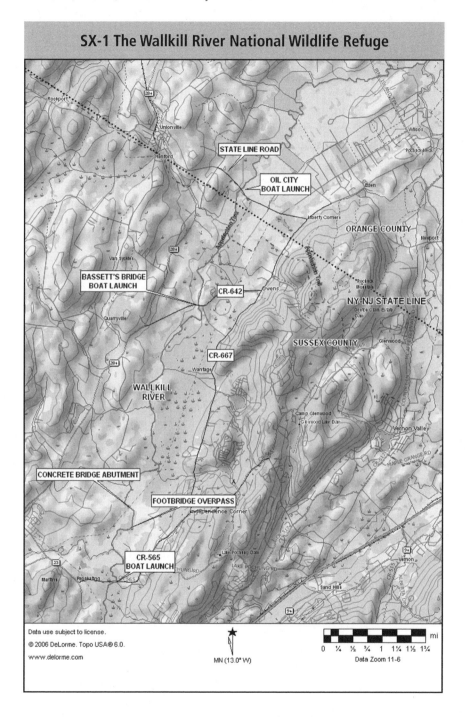

Data use subject to license.

© 2006 DeLorme. Topo USA® 6.0.

www.delorme.com

MN (13.0° W)

0   ¼   ½   ¾   1   1¼ 1½ 1¾   mi

Data Zoom 11-6

Sussex County, NJ

seems less a tool to be employed by man, and more a place simply to be enjoyed.

While the mission of the Refuge System is, in part, the "restoration of the fish, wildlife, and plant resources and their habitats," the word "restoration" is, in the case of the Wallkill River, a bit misleading. The river has been altered over the past two or three centuries with its many dams. Mohawk Lake itself is man-made, the result of the construction of the Lake Mohawk Dam. The river has been further changed by the construction of canals that, in order to create land suitable for agriculture, drained this section of southwestern Orange County, an area prone to the Wallkill's constant flooding. There is no way to restore the original ecology of the area. However, the refuge has provided a diverse habitat for a diverse wildlife population.

Directions to Oil City Road launch site:
The official Web site (http://www.fws.gov/northeast/wallkillriver) offers clear driving directions to the refuge headquarters via a variety of routes. On my first visit to the refuge, I put in at Oil City Road. To get there from I-84, get off at Middletown, exit 3. Follow the signs for US-6 West and stay on it for a little over 3.5 miles. Turn left onto State Route 284 (SR-284) for 9 miles. As you leave Unionville and just before you enter New Jersey, turn left onto State Line Road. This becomes Oil City Road in 1.3 miles where it crosses the Wallkill River, though coming from this direction you will not see an Oil City Road sign. Directly after you cross the Wallkill, the pull-off for launching your boat is on your left. The slow movement of the Wallkill River generally allows travel in both directions, so you can plan trips out and back using one vehicle. After the June 2006 flooding, I went from the CR-565 access to Bassett's Bridge and back, and found fighting the northward current manageable but exhausting. So if you want to cover more distance and have a second vehicle available, I'd suggest starting south and paddling north.

Directions to the other launches:
To get to the other, more southern, two launches, continue on SR-284 past State Line Road. Although you cross into New Jersey, the route name does not change. After 3 miles turn left onto Bassett's Bridge Road (CR-642), following signs to the Bassett's Bridge Access. To get to the south-

▶ **The Wallkill River National Wildlife Refuge**

The refuge provides habitat for over two hundred species of birds.
Here a killdeer wades in the Wallkill, foraging.

ernmost launch within the refuge, stay on SR-284 yet another 4 miles. Turn left at the intersection with SR-23, which in less than a mile joins with CR-565. When the routes split, turn left onto CR-565. In less than a mile the road crosses the Wallkill. On your left there is a pull-off from which you can unload. The refuge mows a path down towards the river, but you need to move your car, parking either at the Lake Pochung Road/ CR-565 intersection close to a mile north, or at a pull-off adjacent to the road about a quarter of a mile south.

The Paddle:
Put in and turn right, heading into the heart of the preserve. For the first half mile, the Wallkill winds through grasslands filled with a flurry of activity of swallows and the chittering of red-winged blackbirds. Gradually the fields give way to shrub and woodlands, then reappear occasionally on first one bank, then the other. In less than a mile you come

to a fork. Stay right; the left fork is actually the mouth of the Papakating Creek. A little over half a mile further, a very low footbridge blocks your way—a stop along a walking trail from the refuge headquarters. The bank all the way to the right of the bridge provides an easy portage. Continue north; here the trees along the sides partially shade the river. The footbridge and the white "refuge boundary" markers alongside the river have been the sole signs of civilization since your launch. Thus, half a mile past the footpath, the concrete stanchion protruding in the middle of the river, a relic of an abandoned rail system, seems particularly incongruous. Refuge land borders the river for most of this eleven-mile journey. Now, though, on your left the land is privately owned and opens up, and you can make out some barns and a silo in the distance. A little further and the view is again shielded by the trees and shrubs hugging the river banks. About four and a half miles from where you put in, the river again opens up somewhat and passes through what was, until very recently, private land. There are no structures, no development, no noises of machinery—simply crude, hand-painted signs warning away trespassers from the river. The refuge purchased this land in 2006 and is re-marking the area. The river bends to the left and you return to the more wooded banks of refuge land. It is a mile and half further to the Bassett's Bridge access. Shortly before the bridge, when the water level is low, you encounter a change of elevation in the river of about a foot. This creates a miniature rapids. If you are paddling against the current, you can easily portage around it.

The section of river between Bassett's Bridge and Oil City Road reveals a variety of wildlife and a variety of habitat. On your right you pass grassland that gives way first to sheer rock face and later to flat forest banks. A very vibrant grass edges the woods, forming a thin green border between the river and the forest. As you traverse the northernmost sections of the refuge, you pass in and out of public land, but fortunately even those properties not acquired by the Fish and Wildlife Service are maintained throughout and are tasteful, unobtrusive, and clean. As you approach the Oil City Road bridge and access, you catch occasional glimpses of a marsh on your right. An occasional, though impassable, channel goes off in that direction. The wildlife of the marsh is best observed on foot from a parking lot a bit further down Oil City Road.

▶ **The Wallkill River National Wildlife Refuge**

Helpful Web site:

• http://www.fws.gov/northeast/wallkillriver
 the home page of the Wallkill River National Wildlife Refuge, part
 of the U.S. Fish and Wildlife Service, gives a wealth of information
 about the sanctuary including its history, wildlife, and habitat. It
 tells about all the various activities the reserve offers and gives
 driving directions.

The Wallkill meanders through the refuge with its diverse habitats—
forests, fields, and swamps.

Sussex County, NJ

C, G, R, S, W	Columbia, Greene, and Other Nearby Counties Ponds and Lakes

COLUMBIA COUNTY

C-3 Copake Lake in Copake

■ **How to get there:** Exit the Taconic State Parkway at State Route 23. Take it east for 3.9 miles. Turn right onto County Route 7 (CR-7). A parking area with lake access is at the intersection of CR-7 and Lakeview Road, 3 miles past the turn.

■ **Where to put in:** The launch from this area at the easternmost point of the lake is a little steep but negotiable.

■ **Remarks:** Woods and scattered houses surround the 410-acre lake.

Web sites:

• www.dec.state.ny.us/website/dfwmr/fish/blscolu.html
  for information on specific location, parking and launch facilities.

• www.dec.state.ny.us/website/dfwmr/fish/lakemaps/cpklkmap.pdf
  provides maps as well as information about fish and the acreage and depth of the lake. Though not meant for navigational use, the map gives water surface area, depths, contours, and species of fish found.

C-4 Kinderhook Lake in Niverville

■ **How to get there:** Exit I-90 at US-9 (exit 12 coming from the north, exit B1 from the east or west). Take US-9 South. Just under 2 miles south of I-90, turn left onto Main Street, also called County Route 28 (CR-28). At 1.9 miles, the road crosses the Valatie Kill. The DEC access is right there, with parking to the right of the road.

■ **Where to put in:** Launch from the parking lot and go under CR-28 heading north into the lake itself.

■ **Remarks:** The good-sized lake—350 acres—is congested with cottages, trailers and small houses dotting its perimeter.

Web sites:

• www.dec.state.ny.us/website/dfwmr/fish/blscolu.html
for information on specific location, parking and launch facilities.

• www.dec.state.ny.us/website/dfwmr/fish/lakemaps/kndrlkmap.pdf
provides maps as well as information about fish and the acreage
and depth of the lake. Though not meant for navigational use, the
map gives water surface area, depths, contours, and species of fish
found.

C-5 Lake Taghkanic in Ancram (Lake Taghkanic State Park)

■ **How to get there:** Take the Taconic State Parkway to the park
entrance, one mile south of the State Route 82 exit.
■ **Where to put in:** The park has designated two sites as boat launches,
one at the far end of West Beach, the other at the boat storage area past
East Beach.
■ **Remarks:** Lake Taghkanic State Park, like many other state parks,
imposes a day-use fee from Memorial Day to Labor Day, and thereafter
on weekends. To use your own kayak or canoe, you must purchase the
annual Taconic Region boat permit. In addition to boating, the park
offers swimming, fishing, hunting, and camping. The scenic 168-acre
lake is surrounded by forested hills; the park is developed with beach
houses, cabins, and cottages.

Web sites:

• http://nysparks.state.ny.us/parks/info.asp?parkID=131
gives information about the facilities at Lake Taghkanic State Park.

• www.dec.state.ny.us/website/d fwmr/fish/lakemaps/lktgncmap.
pdf provides maps as well as information about fish and the acreage and depth of the lake. Though not meant for navigational
use, the map gives water surface area, depths, contours, and
species of fish found.

C-6 Queechy Lake in Canaan

■ **How to get there:** From exit B3 on I-90, turn onto State Route 22
  North and stay on it for about 4 miles. Make a left on County Route 30
  (Queechy Lake Drive). Immediately after your turn, you will see the
  pull-off for the lake on your left. Drive .2 mile down the drive to the
  parking area.

■ **Where to put in:** The lake, with a well-maintained dock, is on your
  right as you drive in.

■ **Remarks:** The 141-acre Queechy Lake is pretty and surrounded by hills,
  which are mainly wooded with a handful of houses on the opposite
  shore.

Web sites:

• www.dec.state.ny.us/website/dfwmr/fish/blscolu.html
  for information on specific location, parking and launch facilities.

• www.dec.state.ny.us/website/dfwmr/fish/lakemaps/qchylkmap.pdf
  provides maps as well as information about fish and the acreage
  and depth of the lake. Though not meant for navigational use, the
  map gives water surface area, depths, contours, and species of
  fish found.

GREENE COUNTY

G-4 CD Lane Park in Windham

■ **How to get there:** Take I-87 to exit 21 (Catskill) and turn left following the signs to State Route 23 (SR-23) West. Stay on SR-23 for just under
  22 miles. Turn left onto SR-296. After 1.5 miles, SR-296 turns to the right.
  Continue straight onto County Route 40 (CR-40), following it for 2 miles.
  Make a left onto CR-56. The park is 1.2 miles ahead on your left.

■ **Where to put in:** Recreational fields lie to the left of the entrance.
  Bear right and park near the pond. Access is easy.

■ **Remarks:** Though it is situated in the Catskill Mountains, the terrain
  surrounding the park does not have the feel of wilderness. The small but
  pretty park, managed by the town of Windham, offers swimming, boat-

▶ **Columbia, Greene, and Other Nearby Counties—Ponds and Lakes**

ing, basketball, and recreational fields. The surrounding area is semi-developed with a scattering of distant houses against the backdrop of more distant mountains. The tiny pond—only 7 acres—was created for recreational use by diverting the Batavia Kill.

G-5 Colgate Lake in East Jewett

■ **How to get there:**
From the south, get off I-87 at exit 20, Saugerties. Make a left onto State Route 212 (SR-212) and a quick right onto SR-32 North. After 6 miles, bear left onto SR-32A for 1.7 miles. Turn left where it ends at SR-23A. Stay on SR-23A West for 5.5 miles, turning right onto County Route 25 (CR-25). Just under 3 miles, bear right onto SR-23C West toward East Jewett. Continue 1 mile, then turn right onto Colgate Road. The lake is 1.4 miles down the road on your right.
From the north, take the New York State Thruway to exit 21, Catskill. Make a left turn onto CR-23B and then go onto SR-23 West. Take the first left after the Thruway onto CR-47—Cauterskill Road—and then the second right onto Vedder Mountain Road. After 2.4 miles, Vedder Mountain Road ends. Turn right onto Cauterskill Road. At a fork in less than a mile, veer left onto Underhill Road, which ends in a little over a mile at SR-23A. Turn right. Stay on SR-23A for 10.5 miles. Turn right onto CR-25. Just under 3 miles, bear right onto SR-23C West toward East Jewett. Continue 1 mile, then turn right onto Colgate Road. The lake is 1.4 miles down the road on your right.
■ **Where to put in:** Access to the lake is easy from the small parking lot.
■ **Remarks:** Nestled against low mountains, this 27-acre lake is beautifully situated in the Catskill Forest Preserve.

Web site:
• http://www.dec.state.ny.us/website/dfwmr/fish/lakemaps/clgtlk-map.pdf provides maps as well as information about fish and the acreage and depth of the lake. Though not meant for navigational use, the map gives water surface area, depths, contours, and species of fish found.

G-6 Green Lake in Athens

■ **How to get there:** Get off I-87 at exit 21, Catskill. At end of exit ramp turn right onto County Route 23B (CR-23B) and continue a little over a mile into the village of Leeds. Turn right on CR-49 (Green Lake Road). Follow the road 2.3 miles to Green Lake. Turn right onto Valley Road. A small park on your left offers lake access.
■ **Where to put in:** From the parking area access is easy.
■ **Remarks:** The area around the 39-acre lake is mainly wooded, but a few houses are always visible. A resort faces the lake directly across from the boat launch. A marsh lies on the northern side of the lake, east of the resort.

Web sites:

• www.dec.state.ny.us/website/dfwmr/fish/blsgree.html
for information on specific location, parking and launch facilities.

• http://www.dec.state.ny.us/website/dfwmr/fish/lakemaps/greenlkmap. pdf provides maps as well as information about fish and the acreage and depth of the lake. Though not meant for navigational use, the map gives water surface area, depths, contours, and species of fish found.

G-7 North-South Lake in Haines Falls

■ **How to get there:** From the south, exit I-87 at exit 20, Saugerties. Turn left at State Route 212 (SR-212), then right onto SR-32 North for 6 miles. Bear left onto SR-32A for 1.7 miles. The road ends at SR-23A. Turn left. Stay on SR-23A West for 5 miles. Turn right onto County Route 18 (CR-18), also called North Lake Road. The road ends 2.2 miles ahead at the lake. (From the north, take the New York State Thruway to exit 21, Catskill. Make a left turn onto CR-23B and then go onto SR-23 West. Take the first left after the Thruway onto CR-47—Cauterskill Road—and then the second right onto Vedder Mountain Road. After 2.4 miles, Vedder Mountain Road ends. Turn right onto Cauterskill Road. At a fork in less than a mile, veer left onto Underhill Road, which ends in a little over a mile at SR-23A. Turn right. Stay on SR-23A for 9.8 miles to CR-18. Turn right.)

▶ **Columbia, Greene, and Other Nearby Counties—Ponds and Lakes**

■ **Where to put in:** There are two official launches, one near the boat rental kiosk on South Lake, the other by the beach on North Lake.

■ **Remarks:** North-South Lake is a DEC-managed campground, the largest in the Catskill Forest Preserve. The two adjoining lakes offer swimming and fishing. The 84-acre lake is situated against a backdrop of cliffs, and short hiking trails lead to impressive views of the area. There is a modest daily use fee.

Web sites:

• www.dec.state.ny.us/website/dfwmr/fish/blsgree.html
for information on specific location, parking and launch facilities.

• www.dec.state.ny.us/website/dfwmr/fish/lakemaps/nslkmap.pdf
provides maps as well as information about fish and the acreage and depth of the lake. Though not meant for navigational use, the map gives water surface area, depths, contours, and species of fish found.

ROCKLAND COUNTY

R-1 Lake Sebago in Pomona (Harriman State Park)

■ **How to get there:**
From the south, take I-87 to exit 15A. Get onto State Route 17 North. Make your first right (2.8 miles) onto Seven Lakes Drive, heading northeast. The lake is 3.5 miles ahead on your left.
From the north, take I-87 to exit 16. Turn left at light and follow the signs for US-6 East. Stay on US-6 for 6.4 miles. Turn right onto Seven Lakes Drive, heading southwest. The lake is about 10 miles ahead on your right.

■ **Where to put in:** The boat launch is, at most, half a mile north of the point where the lake meets the road. On the left side of the parking lot, a concrete ramp leads to the edge of the lake, allowing for an easy launch.

■ **Remarks:** Lake Sebago is part of Harriman State Park. Boating requires purchase of an annual Palisades Interstate Park Commission boat permit. In addition to fishing and boating, the 294-acre lake, surrounded by woods, has a beach area for swimming.

Web sites:

• www.dec.state.ny.us/website/dfwmr/fish/blsrock.html
  for information on specific location, parking and launch facilities.

• www.dec.state.ny.us/website/dfwmr/fish/lakemaps/lksebamap.pdf
  provides maps as well as information about fish and the acreage
  and depth of the lake. Though not meant for navigational use, the
  map gives water surface area, depths, contours, and species of
  fish found.

• http://nysparks.state.ny.us/parks/info.asp?parkID=143
  gives information about the facilities at Harriman State Park.

• http://nysparks.state.ny.us/parks/info.asp?parkID=71
  gives specific information about Lake Sebago.

R-2 Lake Welch in Stony Point (Harriman State Park)

■ **How to get there:**
  From the south, take I-87 to exit 15A. Get onto State Route 17 (SR-
  17) North. Take your first right (2.8 miles) onto Seven Lakes Drive, head-
  ing northeast. Seven miles ahead turn right onto SR-106 East. SR-106
  crosses over the southern portion of the lake 1.75 miles ahead.
  From the north, take I-87 to exit 16. Turn left at light and follow the
  signs for US-6 East. Stay on US-6 for 6.4 miles. Turn right onto Seven
  Lakes Drive, heading southwest for 6.9 miles. Turn left onto SR-106 East.
  SR-106 crosses over the southern portion of the lake 1.75 miles ahead.
■ **Where to put in:** The boat launch is located on the north side of
  County Route 106, a few hundred feet west of the point where the road
  crosses the southernmost portion of the lake. Drive down the entrance
  road almost to the edge of the lake. A gentle slope lends itself to easy
  access.
■ **Remarks:** As with the other lakes in Harriman State Park, boat use
  requires an annual permit. Entrance to the access is locked, so in addition, boaters must rent a key. The 205-acre lake is set against a backdrop
  of wooded hills and low mountains and offers a swimming area in addition to the boat access.

▶ **Columbia, Greene, and Other Nearby Counties—Ponds and Lakes**

Web sites:
- www.dec.state.ny.us/website/dfwmr/fish/blsrock.html
  for information on specific location, parking and launch facilities.

- www.dec.state.ny.us/website/dfwmr/fish/lakemaps/lkwlchmap.pdf
  provides maps as well as information about fish and the acreage
  and depth of the lake. Though not meant for navigational use, the
  map gives water surface area, depths, contours, and species of fish
  found.

- http://nysparks.state.ny.us/parks/info.asp?parkID=143
  gives information about the facilities at Harriman State Park.

- http://nysparks.state.ny.us/parks/info.asp?parkID=74
  gives specific information about Lake Welch.

SULLIVAN COUNTY

S-2 Mongaup Falls Reservoir in Forestburgh

■ **How to get there:** From State Route 17 (SR-17 and future I-86), take
exit 105. Head south on SR-42 for 9.5 miles. The reservoir is 1.9 miles to
the west of SR-42 on Forestburgh Road (County Route 43).

■ **Where to put in:** On your left the DEC access to the reservoir is clearly
marked. A ramp for loading and unloading boats leads down to the
water's edge.

■ **Remarks:** According to locals with whom I spoke, the 129-acre reservoir formerly belonged to Orange and Rockland Utilities. A series of
dams created several reservoirs, and the spillways were used for generat-
ing power. Now the Mongaup Valley Wildlife Management Area admin-
isters much of the land surrounding the reservoir. Signs warn that from
the beginning of December to the end of March the use of the area is
restricted for the protection of endangered species. Eagles winter here.

Web sites:
- www.dec.state.ny.us/website/dfwmr/fish/blssull.html
  for information on specific location, parking and launch facilities.

- www.dec.state.ny.us/website/dfwmr/fish/lakemaps/mongresmap.
pdf provides maps as well as information about fish and the acreage and depth of the lake. Though not meant for navigational use, the map gives water surface area, depths, contours, and species of fish found.

S-3 Rio Reservoir in Forestburgh

■ **How to get there:** From State Route 17 (SR-17 and future I-86), take exit 105. Head south on SR-42 for 9.5 miles, turning right onto Forestburgh Road (County Route 43). Just over half a mile, turn left onto Plank Road and follow it for 2 miles. The Mongaup Valley Wildlife Management Area sign is clearly visible on your right. This access has ample parking and easy access to the reservoir. A second access is located on the southern tip of the dam on Rio Dam Road. To get there, continue south on Plank Road another 2.5 miles. Turn right onto Rio Dam Road. In a little over a mile, the road becomes one lane and goes over the dam. A small parking area is on your right, just past the dam.

■ **Where to put in:** Both the northern and southern launches provide easy access down to the reservoir, near parking.

■ **Remarks:** The Middle Mongaup River runs south to the Delaware, and this beautiful 435-acre reservoir, like the Mongaup Falls Reservoir, lies right in its path. This, too, is a prime place for eagle viewing. The reservoir allows for a 6-plus-mile paddle from a dilapidated wooden bridge at the northern end to the dam at the bottom and then back. After Swinging Bridge Dam upriver developed a sinkhole in May 2005, the water level has been lowered significantly. Current work on the dam by Mirant Corporation, the company that owns Swinging Bridge Reservoir as well as Mongaup Falls Reservoir and Rio Reservoir, promises to ensure the restoration of the dam.

Web sites:
- www.dec.state.ny.us/website/dfwmr/fish/blssull.html
for information on specific location, parking and launch facilities.

- www.dec.state.ny.us/website/dfwmr/fish/lakemaps/rioresmap.pdf
provides maps as well as information about fish and the acreage

▶ **Columbia, Greene, and Other Nearby Counties—Ponds and Lakes**

and depth of the lake. Though not meant for navigational use, the map gives water surface area, depths, contours, and species of fish found.

WESTCHESTER COUNTY

W-1 Mohansic Lake in Yorktown Heights (Franklin D. Roosevelt State Park)

■ **How to get there:** Take the Taconic State Parkway. Get off at Franklin D. Roosevelt State Park exit.
■ **Where to put in:** As you enter the park, keep bearing right towards the pool. Turn right down the driveway marked "Restricted area. Boat permit holders only." The driveway leads to an easy launch. Park your vehicle along the shoulder of the access road.
■ **Remarks:** The 106-acre Mohansic Lake lies within Franklin D. Roosevelt State Park (formerly known as Mohansic State Park). Woods and some lawn surround the lake, giving it a bit of a manicured feel. An annual boat permit is required and provides access to any of a number of Taconic Region state park lakes.

Web sites:
• www.dec.state.ny.us/website/dfwmr/fish/blswest.html
  for information on specific location, parking and launch facilities.

• www.dec.state.ny.us/website/dfwmr/fish/lakemaps/mohalkmap.pdf
  provides maps as well as information about fish and the acreage and depth of the lake. Though not meant for navigational use, the map gives water surface area, depths, contours, and species of fish found.

• http://nysparks.state.ny.us/parks/info.asp?parkID=139
  gives information about the facilities at Franklin D. Roosevelt State Park.

Appendix A: Current Events
Annual Festivities along Hudson RIver Valley Waterways

Hudson River Eagle Fest: The second Sunday in February, Teatown Lake Reservation, a nature preserve and education center in Ossining, sponsors an event celebrating the winter return of the eagle to the area. Participants join naturalists with spotter scopes at several sites along the Hudson River. www.teatown.org

Great River Sweep: Each April since 1998 communities and individuals have joined together for one week to clean up the Hudson River, its tributaries and the shoreline. Scenic Hudson, the former sponsor of the event, provides clean-up kits for volunteers. Volunteer to join a group participating in the event or organize your community to share in the effort. http://ga4.org/scenichudson/DIYgrsguide.html

The Wappinger Creek Water Derby: The New England Canoe and Kayak Racing Association conducts a number of races in late April. www.necanoe.org/

Shad Festivals: Shad, which spend most of their lives in the ocean, swim into the Hudson every spring. Since they spend such a small percentage of their lives in the river, they are one of the only fish considered safe to eat, unaffected by PCBs and other pollutants in the river. When the shad run in late April and May, communities up and down the river celebrate. The Hudson River Foundation for Science and Environmental Research sponsors many of these festivities, including ones in New York City, Fort Lee, Nyack, Croton-on-Hudson, and Catskill. www.hudsonriver.org

The Shad Festival at Boscobel: As a major fund-raising event, Riverkeeper sponsors the mother of all shad festivals at the Boscobel Restoration in Cold Spring. Though pricey, it includes music featuring name bands and "yoga for children, boat building, kayaking lessons, fly fishing, landscape photography, harnessed tree climbing, and a variety of environmentally themed arts and crafts." www.riverkeeper.org/events_index.php

As crowds cheer on the New Paltz Regatta from the SR-299 overpass, swimmers and paddlers join the frolicking crews of the homemade boats.

The New Paltz Regatta: In May on the Wallkill River, the community of New Paltz sponsors a frolicsome rally for homemade boats. www.newpaltz.org/regatta

The ADK Paddlefest at Plum Point: The Adirondack Mountain Club and Hudson Valley Pack and Paddle jointly sponsor a day of activities for both novice and experienced paddlers in mid-May. www.midhudsonadk.org/index.htm or www.hvpackandpaddle.com

Hudson River Greenland Festival: In late May a local outfitter, Hudson Valley Pack and Paddle, hosts a competition of traditional kayaking skills at Norrie Point on the Hudson River to promote Greenland kayaking. Contestants race in streamlined boats handcrafted from wood, and use a slim, more wind-resistant paddle. The festival includes demos and exhibitions as well as contests in Eskimo rolling and races with both paddling and portages. Participants and spectators are welcome. www.hvpackandpaddle.com/Events.htm

The Clearwater Festival: In mid-June, the Clearwater holds a major event celebrating what it calls *the Great Hudson River Revival*. The festival is a full weekend of music, crafts, food, water activities including swimming, seining, sailing, and kayaking, all coupled with environmental education and activism. www.clearwater.org/festival.html

Rip Van Winkle's Wacky Raft Race: In early summer the Ulster-Greene ARC Foundation, a regional organization that raises money to help serve people with developmental disabilities, sponsors a fun-filled benefit. Contestants are invited to float their wacky rafts from Athens to Catskill Point. Spectators also are welcome to join the frivolity with vendors, food and entertainment. www.greenetourism.com

Athens Street Festival: Held in the village of Athens annually in early-to-mid July and billed as "the greatest street festival on the river," the all-day-long festival features an antique and classic car show, crafts, food, children's rides and games, puppet shows, live entertainment, lighthouse tours, Hudson River boat rides, fireworks, and lots more. www.athensstreetfestival.com

The Great Hudson River Paddle: Over a ten-day period in July, a group of hardy paddlers start in Albany and kayak the Hudson River to New York City, camping next to the river. Several local Hudson River outfitters sponsor shorter paddles—from one to three days—that join them. Various exciting events are planned along the way as they pass by. This event is co-sponsored by the Hudson River Valley Greenway, the Hudson River Watertrail Association, and the Hudson River Valley National Heritage Area. www.hrwa.org/ghrp/index.html

The Great Newburgh to Beacon Hudson River Swim: Riverpool in Beacon sponsors a benefit swim across the Hudson River in late July. For safety reasons a contingent of kayaks accompanies the swimmers. The goal of Riverpool is to build at Riverfront Park in Beacon a floating swimming pool open to the river flow. Hoping to serve as a

Towards the end of the seventh day of the Great Hudson River Paddle,
more than thirty kayaks paddle under the Bear Mountain Bridge.

model for others along the Hudson, this initiative celebrates the cleanup of the Hudson River and a return to its recreational use as a safe place to swim. www.riverpool.org/index.html

Esopus Bend Kayak Day: This late July event, jointly sponsored by Upper Hudson River Alliance and the Esopus Creek Conservancy, offers the public a free, full day of kayaking activities in Saugerties, including instruction at both beginner and advanced levels and guided tours of the wetlands on the shores of the creek at Esopus Bend. www.esopuscreekconservancy.org or www.atkenco.com/events.html

Rhinecliff Waterfront Day 2006: This fledgling annual event features kayak races, river rides, water displays, games, venders, and kids' activities during the first week of August. www.hudsonrivervalley.com

Between the Tides Festival: The Saugerties Lighthouse Conservancy sponsors a music fest in mid-August to celebrate the Hudson River and to support the preservation of the lighthouse. It offers live music, square dancing, food, drinks, swimming, and lighthouse tours. www.saugertieslighthouse.com/dayuse/sp_events.shtml

Go Zero Kayak Races: Promoting the use of zero-emission boating on the Hudson River, Scenic Hudson, Foss Group Beacon, and Upper Hudson River Alliance have launched a summer program of long and short-course kayak competitions on the river. The first race takes place in mid-August in Hudson; a second in mid-September in Beacon. www.johnnymilleradventures.com/ or http://gozero.info./files/2006/Vision.pdf

Hudson River Arts Festival: In mid-September the Bardavon Opera House in Poughkeepsie, a theater that presents music, film, dance, and community events, sponsors an annual fall festival featuring nonstop music, folk arts, river cruises, food and fireworks. www.bardavon.org

Hudson River Valley Ramble: This annual gala spans two weekends in September with activities all over the Hudson Valley from Albany to New York. Events highlight the history, culture and ecology of both the valley and the river. They include guided tours of museums, historic sites, walks, hikes, sails, bike trips, canoe trips and kayak trips. www.hudsonriverramble.com

Irma Sagazie Esopus Creek Safari: At the end of September, Esopus Creek Conservancy and Kenco Sports Outfitters co-sponsor a flatwater fund-raising event in Saugerties with kayak and canoe races for both novices and accomplished paddlers. www.esopuscreekconservancy.org

▶ **Appendix A**

Appendix B:
Tours Offered by Environmental Organizations

Audubon New York naturalists lead canoe and kayak tours of the following areas:

- **Constitution Marsh**—a little over eight miles south of the Newburgh-Beacon Bridge, a mile or two north of West Point. Canoe through the marshes of this tidal wetland guided by a naturalist. For additional information, current fees, and reservations, visit the web site at http://ny.audubon.org/cmaccanoe.htm or call (845) 265-2601. (Putnam County)

- **RamsHorn-Livingston Sanctuary**—minutes from the Rip Van Winkle Bridge in Catskill. A naturalist will point out eagles and other wildlife as you paddle through the creek to the Hudson. Visit the web site at http://ny.audubon.org/RamsHorn_paddles.htm or call (518) 678-3248 for further information, current fees and reservations. (Greene County)

Forsyth Nature Center in Kingston offers the following naturalist-led kayak programs during the summer months:

- Friday morning paddles on the Hudson provide the best opportunity for wildlife watching.

- Paddle weekends on the Hudson River; observe and identify birds and aquatic plants.

- Paddle from Kingston Point Beach up the Rondout Creek as you learn the history and the natural history of the area.

All these programs are open to the public. While you may bring your own kayak, rentals are available. Check out the web site at www.forsyth-naturecenter.org or call (845) 331-1682, ext 132 for information, fees and reservations.

FrOGS (Friends of the Great Swamp), a conservation group protecting the Great Swamp in Putnam and Dutchess counties, offers the following paddling trips:

- On two spring weekends (both Saturday and Sunday) two-to-three-hour canoe trips guided by local naturalists leave from Green Chimneys.

- Occasionally FrOGS offers naturalist-led safaris, all-day canoe trips from Patterson to Green Chimneys.

These programs are all open to the public. Visit the Web site at www.frogs-ny.org for specific information about times, fees and reservations.

HRNERR (Hudson River National Estuarine Research Reserve) and NYSDEC (New York State Department of Environmental Conservation) jointly conduct free canoe tours led by naturalists and open to the public at the following sites:

- **Iona Island Marsh**—one mile south of the Bear Mountain Bridge on State Route 9W. Paddle through channels of cattails and common reed out towards Iona Island in the Hudson River. (Rockland County)

- **Stockport Flats**—a few miles north of Hudson. Explore the mouth of Stockport Creek and an island with a beach while you learn about the tidal wetlands. (Columbia County)

- **Tivoli Bays**—three or four miles north of the Kingston-Rhinecliff Bridge. Canoe through the mazelike channels of North Bay. (Dutchess County)

The three-to-four-hour-long tours focus on the ecology of the tidal areas and the importance of protecting our wetlands. Check their Web site at www.dec.state.ny.us/website/hudson/calendar or call (845) 758-7016 for information and reservations.

Appendix C: Tours and Equipment from Private Outfitters

A number of private outfitters in the region rent equipment and lead tours as well. The following is a list of local, private outfitters dedicated primarily to kayaks, kayak accessories and kayak touring.

Columbia County:

Mountain Buddies

17 North Fourth Street, Hudson, NY 12534   (518) 671-6270
www.mountainbuddies.com
www.outdoorpursuits.us is the Web site for their guide service.
Mountain Buddies, one of the newest outfitters in the region, is a full-service outdoor store selling kayaks, accessories and clothing. They also offer Hudson River tours.

Steiner's Sports

301 Warren St., Hudson, NY 12534   (518) 828-5063
3455 Rte 9, Valatie, NY 12184   (518) 784-3663
www.steinerssports.com
Steiner's Sports, with two locations in Columbia County, sells a wide range of rec- reational and touring kayaks, accessories and outdoor clothing. They offer regularly scheduled demo days so equipment can be tested.

Dutchess County:

Hudson Valley Pack and Paddle

45 Beekman Street, Beacon, NY 12508   (845) 831-1300
www.hvpackandpaddle.com
Hudson Valley Pack and Paddle sells kayaks, canoes, and backpacking, climbing, and hiking equipment. They offer rentals, tours, lessons, and boat repair.

The River Connection

9 West Market Street, Hyde Park, NY 12538
(845) 229-0595 or (845) 242-4731
www.the-river-connection.com
Utilizing their high-end equipment, The River Connection offers courses in all levels of

kayaking, taught by instructors certified by the American Canoe Association, and leads tours on the Hudson and its tributaries. Their retail store sells boats and accessories.

Greene County:

Riverview Boat Rentals
103 Main Street, Catskill, NY 12414   (518) 943-5342
www.riverviewmarineservices.com
Riverview Boat Rentals is a full-service marina located on the Catskill Creek. In addition to their fleet of powerboats and sailboats, they rent recreational kayaks and canoes with easy access to the Hudson River and RamsHorn-Livingston Sanctuary.

Orange County:

Mountain Valley Guides
New Windsor, NY 12553   (845) 661-1923
www.mountainvalleyguides.com
Mountain Valley Guides offers clinics and guided trips on the Hudson River, especially in the Plum Point, Moodna Creek, Bannerman Island area, and multi-day kayak-camping trips in the Adirondacks.

Putnam County:

Hudson Valley Outfitters
63 Main Street, Cold Spring NY 10516   (845) 265-0221
www.hudsonvalleyoutfitters.com
Hudson Valley Outfitters specializes in kayak sales, rentals, lessons, and tours on the Hudson River.

Fox Lane Boatworks
11 Fields Lane, Brewster, NY 10509   (845) 278-0647
http://www.foxlaneboatworks.com
Fox Lane Boatworks offers both Hudson River and Long Island Sound tours and lessons with a certified instructor. In addition they offer boat building workshops as well as a summer boat building program for teens.

▶ **Appendix C**

Rockland County:

Matt's Sporting Goods
57 Route 9W, Haverstraw, NY 10927   (845) 429-3254

Matt's Sporting Goods, one of the oldest paddle shops in the state, carries a complete line of kayaks, accessories and clothing. As its name suggests, the store caters to several sports. Their knowledge about fishing has led to their emergence as a leading retailer for the new and fast-growing sport of kayak-fishing.

Ulster County:

Atlantic Kayak Tours
320 West Saugerties Road, Saugerties, New York 12477
(845) 245-2187   www.atlantickayaktours.com

Atlantic Kayak Tours leads a variety of trips at all levels of expertise exploring not only the Hudson River, but Connecticut rivers, the New York Harbor, and the Long Island Sound as well. In addition they offer instruction, sales, and rentals of kayaks and canoes. They operate kayak centers from state land at both Annsville Creek and Norrie Point.

Cold Brook Canoes
4181 Route 28, Box 43, Boiceville, NY 12412   (845) 657-2189

Cold Brook Canoes, a family-owned business since 1970 run by octogenarian, flatwater enthusiast, Ernie Gardner, sells a wide range of kayaks and canoes as well as accessories.

Kenco
1000 Hurley Mountain Rd., Kingston, NY 12401
(845) 340-0552 or (800) 872-2964
www.atkenco.com or www.nykayaks.com for information on river tours.

Kenco sells a full line of recreational and touring kayaks, canoes, and accessories including roof racks. They offer daily rentals, lessons at all skill levels, and Hudson River and Rondout Creek kayak tours.

Westchester County:

American Terrain, Inc.

175 East Post Road, White Plains, NY 10601   (914) 682-3971
www.americanterrain.com

American Terrain is a retail store for the outdoor enthusiast. In addition to selling accessories and clothing, they boast one of the largest selections of kayaks in Westchester County. They also offer demo days allowing customers to try before they buy.

Atlantic Kayak Tours at Annsville Creek Paddlesport Center

Hudson Highlands State Park, Route 6 & 202, Annsville Circle
Cortlandt Manor, NY 10567   (914) 739-2588
www.paddlesportcenter.com

Atlantic Kayak Tours leads a variety of trips at all levels of expertise, exploring not only the Hudson River, but Connecticut rivers, the New York Harbor, and the Long Island Sound as well. In addition they offer instruction, sales, and rentals of kayaks and canoes. They operate kayak centers from state land at both Annsville Creek in Westchester and Norrie Point in Dutchess County.

Hudson River Recreation

247 Palmer Avenue, Sleepy Hollow, NY 10591   (914) 524-0046
www.kayakhudson.com

From three starting points—New Rochelle, Nyack and Sleepy Hollow—Hudson River Recreation leads a variety of Hudson River and Long Island Sound tours, including a popular moonlight excursion. They also offer instructional programs, including special courses for women and for teens.

Jagger's Camp & Trail Outfitters

359 Adams Street, Bedford Hills, NY 10506   (914) 241-4448
www.jaggerscamptrail.com

Jagger's Camp and Trail Outfitters is a retail store that sells a variety of recreational canoes and kayaks and outdoor clothing.

Glossary

access place for putting the kayak into or taking the kayak out of the water

brackish somewhat salty—less salty than the ocean—brackish water is usually found where seawater and freshwater meet

channel narrow passage through vegetation or other obstructions in the water

class I-VI international classification system for rating white water (class I nominal current, class VI extremely turbulent)

deadfall fallen trees and branches obstructing the course of river or creek

downriver in the direction of the current; toward the mouth of the river

downstream in the direction of the current; with the current

estuary a river, like the Hudson, affected by both tides and current, where salt and freshwater mix

flat water calm water with no discernible current or choppiness

gradient the rate of descent of a river or creek (the gradient affects the current)

kill stream or creek

launch put boat into water; the place from which boat is put into water

moving flat water water with a decided current but no rapids

outfitter company supplying equipment for kayaking (and other outdoor recreation)

PFD life jacket (short for personal flotation device)

portage carrying kayak and gear around an obstacle or from one body of water to another

put-in place of entry into waterway

rapids portion of river or creek characterized by fast current often combined with obstructions

riffles slight rapids caused by current flowing over shallow bottom

take-out place for exiting waterway

tidal caused or influenced by tides; the Hudson River is tidal, the current determined by Atlantic Ocean tides rather than the southward flow from its headwaters

upriver away from the current; in the direction of the source of the river

upstream away from the flow of the current; against the current

white water stretch of water characterized by a succession of rapids

For Further Information

Recommended Books

Giddy, Ian H. and the Hudson River Watertrail Association. *The Hudson River Water Trail Guide—A River Guide for Small Boaters.* New York: Hudson River Watertrail Association, 2003. This is the ultimate guide for small boating on the lower, tidal portion of the Hudson River from Troy to New York City. Primarily it offers detailed descriptions of the river, including launches, islands, beaches, creeks, points, parks, historic sites, architectural sites, marinas, and train stations. Supplementing this is valuable information on the science of the region, with sections on its geology and its ecosystems, and safety considerations including a chapter on tides and currents.

Hayes, John and Alex Wilson. *Quiet Water—Canoe Guide—New York—Best Paddling Lakes and Ponds for Canoe and Kayak.* The title speaks for itself. The recommended places are strictly flatwater and located all over the state. If you are prepared to travel distances in search of a pristine lake, this is a great guide.

Squires, Dennis. *New York Exposed—The Whitewater State—Volume 2—The whitewater guide of south flowing rivers in New York State—the drainages of the Hudson River, and the Delaware River.* New York: A White Water Outlaw Publishing, 2003. If you decide to move on from flat water to white water, you will find Dennis Squires' book useful with its descriptions of over 90 sections of rivers. Volume 2 covers the waterways in the Hudson River Valley region.

Recommended Web sites

For information about where to kayak:

http://www.dec.state.ny.us/website/dfwmr/fish/foe4cbl1.html is a DEC site listing the counties of New York. Click on a county and get all the official DEC launch sites with the location, type of launch, and amount of available parking.

http://www.acanet.org/recreation/watertrails.lasso has compiled a searchable list of all the water trails throughout the United States.

For information about specific rivers:

http://www.amc-ny.org/recreational-activities/canoe/riverinfo.shtml is a site maintained by the Appalachian Mountain Club that gives data on sections of eastern rivers from West Virginia to Maine. The information includes class, an international scale for measuring difficulty of white water.

http://newweb.erh.noaa.gov/ahps2/index.php?wfo=aly is a government Web site providing up-to-date information about area rivers at particular locations, including current and flood-stage depths.

For information about outdoor activities in the Catskill Mountain region:

http://www.catskillmountainclub.org/index.html is the Web site of the Catskill Mountain Club. The Web site gives information about all types of outdoor activities within the Catskill State Park.

For information about governmental agencies and not-for-profit groups working to protect the environment:

http://www.thebeaconinstitute.org is the home site of the Beacon Institute, an organization whose mission involves establishing a center for research, policy-making and education about estuaries and rivers, and the relationship between them and society at large.

http://www.clearwater.org is the Web site of Clearwater, the environmental group that has as its mission the protection and preservation of the Hudson River and its communities. The site has a wealth of information about environmental issues, environmental education, the Sloop Clearwater, and the festivals, books, and films the organization sponsors.

http://www.dec.state.ny.us/website/dfwmr/fish/fishmail.html#links is the home site of the DEC Bureau of Fisheries. The site says the Bureau of Fisheries "is typically your best source of information concerning fishing opportunities, fisheries management, stocking, public access and other issues associated with local waters."

http://www.dec.state.ny.us/website/hudson/hrnerr.html is the official Web site of the Hudson River National Estuarine Research Reserve, a federal scientific ini-

▶ **For Further Information**

tiative managed by the New York State Department of Environmental Conservation in cooperation with a slew of other state and interstate agencies, focusing on research and education. As part of their educational mandate, the agency runs a number of interpretative programs open to the public.

http://www.hrwa.org is the Web site of the Hudson River Watertrail Association, whose mission is to establish a water trail from the mouth of the Hudson River all the way to the Great Lakes. They are co-sponsors of the annual Great Hudson River Paddle, and the authors and publishers of *The Hudson River Water Trail Guide.*

http://www.hudsongreenway.state.ny.us is a state agency whose goal is the development and preservation of the Hudson River Valley's scenic, recreational, cultural, and historical resources. Of special note to kayakers, the agency has co-sponsored the Great Hudson River Paddle and has established a 156-mile water trail from Waterford in Saratoga County to Battery in lower Manhattan.

http://www.nature.org is the home site of the Nature Conservancy, an environmental group dedicated to preserving the land and waters needed to support biodiversity. The Nature Conservancy supports its mission through a great variety of nature events and outdoor activities including hikes and kayak and canoe trips.

http://www.riverkeeper.org is the home page of Riverkeeper, one of the foremost environmental groups interested in protecting the water of the Hudson River. They sponsor some events and festivals to celebrate the waterway, most in the New York City area.

http://www.scenichudson.org is the home site of Scenic Hudson, an activist environmental group. The Web site provides information on the preservation of the environment, the cleanup of brownfields, PCBs and other pollutants, and the parks and preserves that it has helped create and/or preserve.

http://www.uhra.us is the Web site of the Upper Hudson River Alliance, an organization dedicated to developing resources involving recreation, culture and heritage within the Upper Hudson Valley, specifically in the towns of Athens, Hudson, Saugerties and Tivoli, and reconnecting the four communities economically with each other and with the river.

Paddles by Body of Water

Rivers and Creeks

Bashakill

The Bashakill (Sullivan)

Black Creek

Black Creek in Lloyd (Ulster)

Chodikee Lake in Highland (Ulster)

Catskill Creek

Catskill Creek in Catskill (Greene)

Dubois Creek into the RamsHorn-Livingston Sanctuary (Greene)

Claverack Creek

Stockport Creek to Claverack and Kinderhook Creeks (Columbia)

Delaware River

Delaware River from Mongaup to Port Jervis (Orange)

Dubois Creek

Dubois Creek into the RamsHorn-Livingston Sanctuary (Greene)

East Branch Croton River

East Branch Croton River—Starting from Green Chimneys (Putnam)

East Branch Croton River from Patterson to Green Chimneys (Putnam)

Esopus Creek

Esopus Creek from the Village of Saugerties towards Kingston (Ulster)

The Mouth of the Esopus Creek in Saugerties (Ulster)

Fishkill Creek

Fishkill Creek in Brinckerhoff (Dutchess)

The Mouth of the Fishkill Creek in Beacon (Dutchess)

Hudson River

Constitution Marsh in Cold Spring (Putnam)

Catskill Creek in Catskill (Greene)

Dubois Creek into the RamsHorn-Livingston Sanctuary (Greene)

Moodna Creek and Marsh in New Windsor (Orange)

RamsHorn Creek into the Rams-Horn-Livingston Sanctuary (Greene)

The Mouth of the Esopus Creek in Saugerties (Ulster)

Tivoli Bays in Red Hook (Dutchess)

Stockport Creek to Claverack and Kinderhook Creeks (Columbia)

Stockport Flats Area (Columbia)

Kinderhook Creek

Stockport Creek to Claverack and Kinderhook Creeks (Columbia)

Moodna Creek

Moodna Creek and Marsh in New Windsor (Orange)

Neversink River

Neversink River from Cuddeback-ville to Matamoras, PA (Orange)

Otter Kill

Otter Kill in Washingtonville (Orange)

RamsHorn Creek

RamsHorn Creek into the Rams-Horn-Livingston Sanctuary (Greene)

Rondout Creek

Rondout Creek in the High Falls Area (Ulster)

Rondout Creek in Eddyville (Ulster)

Rondout Creek in Kingston (Ulster)

Stockport Creek

Stockport Creek to Claverack and Kinderhook Creeks (Columbia)

Tenmile River

Tenmile River from Dover Plains to Webatuck (Dutchess)

Wallkill River

Wallkill River in Warwick (Orange)

Wallkill River from Wallkill to Walden (Ulster)

Wallkill River from New Paltz to Rifton (Ulster)

The Wallkill River National Wildlife Refuge (Sussex)

Wappinger Creek

Wappinger Creek from Pleasant Valley to Poughkeepsie (Dutchess)

The Mouth of the Wappinger Creek in Wappingers Falls (Dutchess)

Ponds and Lakes

Alder Lake in Hardenburgh (Ulster)

Bashakill in Mamakating (Sullivan)

Blue Lake in Warwick (Orange)

Canopus Lake in Philipstown (Putnam)

CD Lane Park in Windham (Greene)

Chodikee Lake in Highland (Ulster)

Colgate Lake in East Jewett (Greene)

Copake Lake in Copake (Columbia)

Green Lake in Athens (Greene)

Island Pond in Tuxedo (Orange)

Kinderhook Lake in Niverville (Columbia)

Lake Askoti in Tuxedo (Orange)

Lake Kanawauke in Tuxedo (Orange)

Lake Minnewaska in Gardiner (Ulster)

Lake Sebago in Pomona (Rockland)

Lake Skannatati in Tuxedo (Orange)

Lake Stahahe in Tuxedo (Orange)

Lake Taghkanic in Ancram (Columbia)

Lake Tiorati in Tuxedo (Orange)

Lake Welch in Stony Point (Rockland)

Little Dam Lake in Tuxedo (Orange)

Mohansic Lake in Yorktown Heights (Westchester)

Mongaup Falls Reservoir in Forestburgh (Sullivan)

North-South Lake in Haines Falls (Greene)

Onteora Lake in Kingston (Ulster)

Queechy Lake in Canaan (Columbia)

Rio Reservoir in Forestburgh (Sullivan)

Rudd Pond at Taconic State Park in Millerton (Dutchess)

Silver Mine Lake in Woodbury (Orange)

Stillwater Pond in Putnam Valley (Putnam)

Stissing Pond in Pine Plains (Dutchess)

Sylvan Lake in Beekman (Dutchess)

Tillson Lake in Gardiner (Ulster)

Upper Pond in Woodstock (Ulster)

Upton Lake in Stanford (Dutchess)

Wappinger Lake in Wappingers Falls (Dutchess)

Winding Hills County Park in Montgomery (Orange)

White Pond in Kent (Putnam)

Yankeetown Pond in Woodstock (Ulster)

About the Author

Shari Aber grew up in New York City, graduated from City College of New York, and taught in public schools in upper Manhattan and the South Bronx. She left the city to raise a family and settled in the Mid-Hudson Valley. After a short hiatus, she resumed her career and taught English for twenty-nine years. She retired from teaching at Newburgh Free Academy in 2005.

Worried at first about leaving the excitement of the city, she learned to appreciate the outdoors and the quiet of the country. At the foot of the Shawangunk Mountains in New Paltz, she and her husband opened a horseback riding stable leading rides through the trails of the eastern Gunks. Though she no longer rides, she still loves the outdoors, spending much of her time hiking, skiing, biking and, most recently, kayaking.

She has written off and on since childhood, publishing short pieces in small presses. This is her first book.